SPECIAL OLYMPICS

THE FIRST 25 YEARS

by Ana Bueno ❖ *Foreword by Rafer Johnson*

Foghorn Press

BOOKS BUILDING COMMUNITY™

ISBN 0-935701-85-0

Foghorn Press titles are distributed to the book trade by
Publishers Group West, Emeryville, California.
To contact your local representative, call 1-800-788-3123.

To order individual books, please call Foghorn Press at
1-800-FOGHORN (364-4676).

Printed in the United States of America.

SPECIAL
OLYMPICS
THE FIRST 25 YEARS

by Ana Bueno ❖ *Foreword by Rafer Johnson*

BOOKS BUILDING COMMUNITY™

Credits

Ana Bueno is a writer who lives in Los Angeles with her husband, David Horwich, and her two dachshunds *Dodger Dog* and *Vienna*. Ana is a longtime volunteer of California Special Olympics.

Managing Editor
Ann Marie Brown

Book Design
Michele Thomas

Associate Editor
Howard Rabinowitz

California Special Olympics provided all of the photographs on the following pages and on the cover of this book.

Acknowledgments

California Special Olympics and Ana Bueno would like to give special thanks and gratitude to the following people who either provided materials, allowed themselves to be interviewed or checked the manuscript for errors of chronology or fact: Rafer Johnson, Greg Bingham, Mikkole Albano, Bill Fields, Kevin Martin, Lisa Freedman, Tom Fitzsimmons, Dick Blankenburg, Madeline Evans, Paul Hoffman, Ed Arnold, Jimmy Johnson and the staff at California Special Olympics and Special Olympics International.

"Let me win, but if I cannot win, let me be brave in the attempt."
Special Olympics Oath

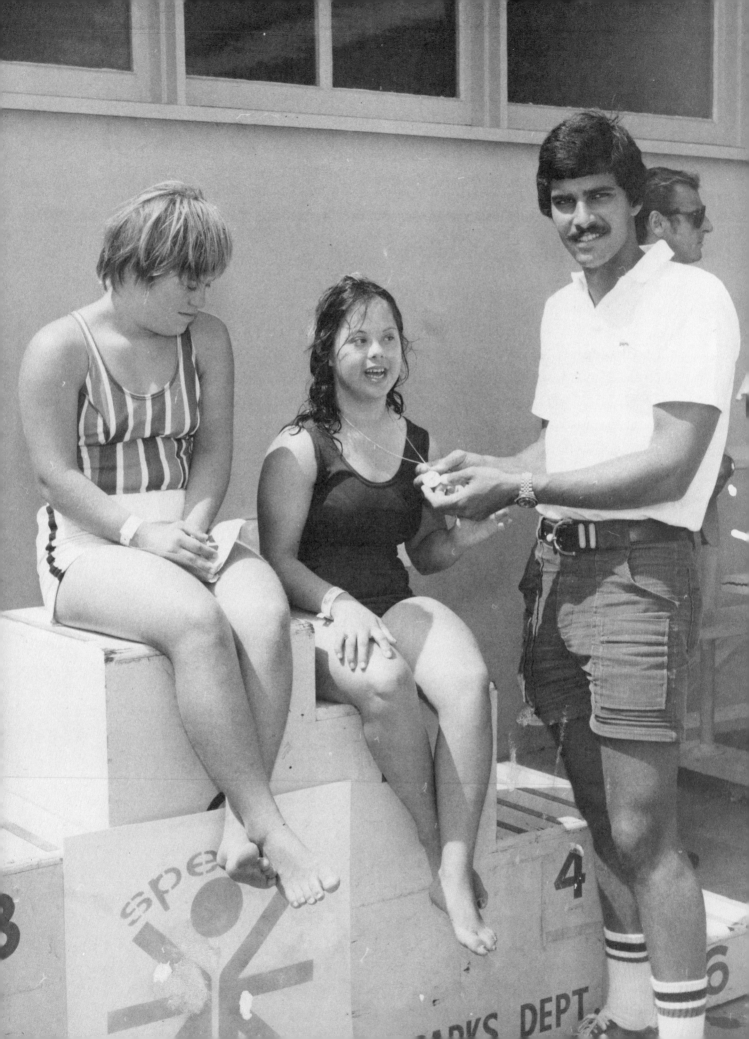

Contents

*OPPOSITE: Olympic swimmer
Mark Spitz joins two Special
Olympians during a 1973
aquatics event.*

Foreword

by Rafer Johnson
1960 Olympic Gold Medalist, Decathlon

Eunice Kennedy Shriver called me in 1968 with an invitation to join her and others in Chicago for the first Special Olympics games. I accepted because I thought it was a great concept and I wanted to be a part of this program of support for children and adults with mental retardation. I saw how little had been done for citizens with mental retardation and knew how much more could be accomplished.

One of my strongest memories from the first Special Olympics games in Chicago in 1968 was a performance by a choral group composed of children with mental retardation from a facility in Canfield, Connecticut. In the film *A Dream to Grow On*, you can see me standing with them in front of City Hall while they sing. After the filming, I spoke with Fran Kelly, the director of the Connecticut facility, about the way they were caring for the children there. Their approach seemed ahead of the times. Well, the thing that got me was this: Here were people who weren't getting all the help they could and yet as a group they had accomplished so much. It really hooked me. I know you can't get where you want without interest from other people. So I just jumped right in. I wanted to help Special Olympics grow. And I am just one of many people doing something for the program because of an experience each one of us had while attending a Special Olympics event.

OPPOSITE: Rafer Johnson applauding the athletes of Special Olympics at the closing ceremonies of the 1991 Summer Games.

I remember growing up as a little kid in central California. My teachers, coaches and friends showed an interest in me and it helped me become what I am. I'm just one of many people who had support and help growing up. My parents, friends, coaches and teachers provided encouragement and taught me to be the best I could be. There were 100 of us in my Kingsburg High School graduating class. We were all so close that when a party was given, all 100 were invited. That's how it was. One for all, all for one.

At an early age, I wanted to be successful. I wanted to be good at school, so I worked hard. Along the way, different coaches at every level helped me. I credit Murl Dodson, my coach at Kingsburg, for the progress I made from one sport to another. I was a sprinter and high jumper. It was Murl Dodson who said I should try the long jump and the hurdles. I wouldn't have been as quick to try those events; but with Coach Dodson's insight and support, I did try them and they turned out to be my best events.

I guess that's one reason I'm a team player; I like to be a part of something where everybody is doing their best to help everyone do better. I ran the last leg of the torch run to open the '84 Olympic Games at the Los Angeles Coliseum and those are feelings and memories I'll never forget. I had to run down a long darkened tunnel to reach the field entrance. As I ran out into the light, I was handed the torch. When I started to run down the track with the torch, I sensed a deep emotional reaching out, a spirit of collaboration, from the Olympian athletes surrounding me. It was as though each and every one of them had their hands on the torch, along with mine. And as I ran up the stairs of the Coliseum to light the Olympic flame, I completed the last leg of a worldwide relay. More than 10,000 people—men, women, boys and girls from big cities, little towns, all sizes, all colors, all countries—had helped relay that flame from Greece to Los Angeles. It was the ultimate team: First leg, middle or last leg, everyone had to do it right. And I was the last leg in that effort. That's the way life ought to be; we all should run our leg of the race with people cheering, helping, everything getting done. It's only going to be good if we all run our leg of the relay well.

There are lots of ways to find success. Hard work is one of them. I worked hard. If I knew I was going to win, it's because I knew I had worked harder. I think the most successful people are those who have someone helping them. If you have someone standing alongside you who wants you to be the best and who knows you—who you are, your strengths, your weaknesses—you will probably progress much further than you thought you could. In team-work, there's much more strength, depth and success. There are two sets of eyes, two sets of hands and two hearts working together.

And that's what I am for special athletes— another set of eyes, another set of hands and a heart working to be there for them, finding a way to help them be the best that they can be. I'm on their team.

Rafer Johnson
Los Angeles, 1994

Prologue

Prologue

This is a story about how personal experience combined with loving kindness helped spark action, a story about reaching beyond fear and prejudice to uncover underlying courage and hidden potential. It's about creating opportunities for people who were once discounted and removed from our community, and about how they are being integrated—mainstreamed—back into society as citizens with something positive to contribute. This is a story of the first 25 years of a movement called Special Olympics.

As defined in its mission statement, Special Olympics is a worldwide organization that provides year-round sports training and competition in a variety of Olympic-type sports for children and adults with mental retardation. The training and competition experienced by these individuals offer them the opportunity to develop physical fitness, as well as the chance to demonstrate courage, experience joy and success, and build stronger relationships with their families, teammates and members of their communities.

Special Olympics is officially recognized and affiliated with the United States Olympic Committee; it is the only other organization in the United States authorized to use the name "Olympics." This affiliation is an honor, acknowledging that the philosophy of Special Olympics is aligned with the Olympic ideal of sportsmanship and love of participation for its own sake. It is also a responsibility, since the rules of Special Olympics competition are

OPPOSITE: One of the early Special Olympics events.

modeled after the principles of training which govern national and international Olympic sport competition.

Every human being is faced with the challenges of achieving some measure of physical fitness, participating in activities that demand courage and building significant interpersonal relationships. Many of us do not even think twice about our abilities to meet these challenges. However, there are some people who not only think about developing these areas of their lives—they concentrate all their energy on doing so. Some are professional athletes and some are special athletes.

Children and adults with mental retardation, the special athletes of Special Olympics, do not have a disease, nor are they mentally ill, experiencing disorders of the mind in the areas of emotion, perception, memory or thought. Nor are all born with mental retardation. Mental retardation can also occur in childhood from brain injury or gross psychological deprivation. Consequently, some causes are preventable or treatable. While there are well over 350 known causes of mental retardation, in three-fourths of the cases, the specific cause is unknown.

The current medical view of mental retardation in relation to cause and treatment incorporates studies that have been prompted by the Joseph P. Kennedy, Jr. Foundation. Today, the most generally accepted technical definition describes mental retardation as "significant sub-average general intellectual functioning existing concurrently with deficits in adaptive behavior and manifested during the developmental period (before age 18)." The primary manifestation is a limited and slower rate of learning. People with mental retardation also have difficulty managing the ordinary activities of daily living, understanding the behavior of others and determining appropriate social responses. (Keep in mind that this depends partially on social circumstances. A person with mental retardation who has difficulty functioning in a complex culture may manage well in a simpler environment.)

In fact, 89 percent of all people with mental retardation have such mild forms that in many respects they are indistinguishable from people who have no developmental handicap. People with mild mental retardation score between 50 and 70 on intelligence quotient (IQ) tests. (In the general population, the average IQ is about 100 with a standard deviation of about 15, meaning that the so-called normal IQ is between 85 and 115.) With education, they frequently function adequately in society. At this level of mental retardation, the psychological environment plays an important role in the person's ability to lead "a successful life." When we say "a successful life," it means just this: that the person is using the full scope of his or her capabilities, discovering and exploiting his or her potential in society.

Many of the children and adults with mental retardation caused by Down syndrome fall into this 89 percent. Once called "mongolism" because it causes a slight, oblique slant of the eyes, Down syndrome (or Trisomy 21, as it is medically named) is caused by a chromosome aberration in which there are three of the Number 21 chromosomes instead of the usual two. People with mental retardation caused by Down syndrome typically score between 50 and 60 on IQ tests. There are also rare partial forms of Down syndrome which occur with a higher IQ level. Education can dramatically alter the course of this handicap—education

not only for people with mental retardation, but also for the public.

People with mental retardation constitute one of the world's largest groups with disabilities. In the United States alone, seven-and-a-half million individuals have mental retardation. Annually, over 125,000 babies are born with mental retardation. In the world, 300 million individuals have mental retardation. Race, education, social and economic factors play no part in the occurrence of mental retardation. It can happen to anyone.

Rosemary Kennedy was born on September 13, 1919, in Brookline, Massachusetts. A beautiful child, she took after her mother, Rose Fitzgerald Kennedy. She appeared to be a little slower than her siblings in learning to crawl, walk and talk, but in a competitive household with two brilliant boys, it seemed unfair to compare her development to theirs. Everyone was certain she would catch up in her own time. But Rosemary never would catch up; she was eventually diagnosed as mentally retarded. No one is sure what exactly caused her mental retardation, nor did it matter, because the decision was made that she belonged in the loving environment of the family household.

This was a bold move at a time when the accepted practice was to place children, even babies, into institutions as soon as it was realized they were mentally retarded. "Feeble-minded," "idiot" and "moron" were actual medical classifications given to levels of retardation at that time. Research time and money were not spent on investigating the causes and prevention of mental retardation. Public opinion was uninformed, negative and tainted with fear. Mental retardation was misunderstood and confused with other afflictions, such

Eunice Kennedy Shriver and Rafer Johnson share a moment during the early 1970s at one of the first International Games in Los Angeles, California.

as mental illness or various brain diseases, which are totally unrelated to developmental disabilities. State institutions, even as late as the 1950s, were dismal holding tanks.

Rosemary, the third child and eldest daughter of Rose and Joseph Patrick Kennedy, grew from a beautiful child into a beautiful woman. She flourished in the warmth and attention of her parents, brothers and sisters. Rosemary loved other children and especially loved her little sister Eunice Mary Kennedy, who was born the fifth of nine Kennedy children. Rose-

mary was included in all family activities, even living with the family in London during the late 1930s while her father was Ambassador of the United States to the Court of St. James'. But as time went on, it became increasingly difficult for Rosemary to continue living at home. In 1942, Rose Kennedy placed Rosemary in a progressive, caring residential facility for exceptional children, St. Coletta's, near Jefferson, Wisconsin.

World War II bought tragedy into the lives of many American families and also into the lives of the Kennedy family. The Joseph P. Kennedy, Jr. Foundation was established in 1946 in loving memory of the Kennedys' eldest son, who was killed while on an air mission on August 12, 1944. This was the first charitable foundation devoted to the benefit of people with mental retardation. In keeping with the Kennedy family's belief, the guiding principle of the Foundation is that the "best investment for social good is in people and the unlimited possibilities of the human mind and spirit."

In its early years, the Foundation built centers for the care of children with mental retardation. Later, when it became apparent there was a need for research, the Foundation funded the establishment of the Kennedy Laboratories at Massachusetts General Hospital, Johns Hopkins and other medical institutions. Amazingly enough, even in the late 1950s, most medical schools did not have instruction and education on the subject of mental retardation. It was Dr. Robert Cook, head of the Johns Hopkins research effort, who prepared the first course of study in mental retardation to be offered at a medical school. The Foundation set out two major objectives: 1) to seek the prevention of mental retardation by identifying its causes; and 2) to improve the means by which society deals with its citizens who have mental retardation.

Raised in a home which was loving and protective of Rosemary, Eunice Kennedy understood the issues that must be faced when a family member is mentally retarded. Rosemary had been living at St. Coletta's for some time when Eunice moved to California to attend and eventually receive her undergraduate degree from Stanford University. Following graduation in 1945, Eunice moved to Washing-

ton, D.C., where she worked for the State Department in the Special War Problems Department. During the late 1940s and into the '50s, Eunice's interests shifted toward juvenile delinquency; she worked as the Coordinator of the National Conference on Prevention and Control of Juvenile Delinquency for the Department of Justice. Later she moved into social work, serving at the Penitentiary for Women in Alderson, West Virginia and later working in Chicago with the House of the Good Shepherd and the Chicago Juvenile Court.

Through all these varied environments, Eunice's interest in the work of the Joseph P. Kennedy, Jr. Foundation never flagged. In 1955, her father asked her help to determine how the Foundation's grants could be utilized best. To research a response to that question, she traveled around the country, talking to experts and visiting the institutions which housed America's most retarded.

"I remember well one state institution we visited," Eunice wrote of the experience years later. "There was an overpowering smell of urine from clothes and from the floors. I remember the retarded patients had nothing to do...I recall other institutions where several thousand adults and children were housed in bleak, overcrowded wards of 100 or more, living out their lives on a dead-end street, unloved, unwanted, some of them strapped in chairs like criminals. There was a complete lack of knowledge about their capacities. They were isolated because their families were embarrassed and the public was prejudiced."

In 1956, at the Olympic Games held in Melbourne, Australia, an outstanding young black athlete from Kingsburg, Califor-

Eunice Kennedy Shriver with her sister-in-law Ethel Kennedy and sister Pat Kennedy Lawford. Special Olympics is a family affair for everyone.

nia by the name of Rafer Johnson won a silver medal in the decathlon. In America's Deep South, the Reverend Martin Luther King, Jr., emerged as a charismatic leader of the Civil Rights movement by taking a strong stand for desegregation. America was poised for change.

In 1957, Eunice Kennedy Shriver assumed direction of the Joseph P. Kennedy, Jr. Foundation, embarking on a course that would change the way people with mental retardation are accepted and treated worldwide. Meanwhile,

another member of the Kennedy family, John Fitzgerald, was also charting a course in new waters—toward the presidency.

At this time, Rafer Johnson was attending the University of California, Los Angeles. Rafer, an athletic talent who naturally combined intellect, leadership and a high regard for teamwork, was preparing for the next Olympic Games, scheduled to be held in 1960 in Rome, Italy. In 1959, while a senior at UCLA and president of the student body,

Team California at the Los Angeles Sports Arena with Rafer Johnson during an L.A. Clippers basketball game.

Rafer had the unique honor to introduce presidential candidate Senator John F. Kennedy to an assembly of fellow students. That day, Kennedy struck a chord in Rafer's heart and mind when he said to the students, "It is time for a new generation of leadership to cope with new problems and new opportunities, for there is a new world to be won."

By the end of 1960, John F. Kennedy had won the presidency, Rafer Johnson had won gold in the Rome Olympics and Eunice Kennedy Shriver had started to plan a campaign to position the cause of persons with mental retardation as a number-one priority for government funding and public attention.

Americans in 1960 witnessed the organization of Students for a Democratic Society, the left-wing student movement started by Mario Salvio at the University of California, Berkeley, which spread to campuses countrywide and instigated the first student protest, a nonviolent sit-in protesting segregation at whites-only lunch counters in Greensboro, North Carolina.

"We stand at the edge of a new frontier—the frontier of the '60s, a frontier of unknown opportunities and peril, a frontier of unfulfilled hopes and threat," John F. Kennedy said at his 1961 inauguration, rallying the people of the United States. His words encapsulated both the optimism and the fear facing Americans on the brink of social change. Civil rights was the most important issue, and it didn't just mean sweeping away the barriers which previously held the black population from full participation in American society. Women, Native Americans and others also began rethinking their proper place in the American dream. Poverty was the enemy and economic parity the goal. Equality was sought in all areas for all people.

The challenges in America were great. Individuals asked themselves what they could do for their country. There was an unprecedented growth in cause-related organizations. Participation in active change was the hallmark of the era. President Kennedy led the way by example. America got the Peace Corps and the space mission—our chance to walk on the moon.

In early 1961, Rafer Johnson was in New York to receive the Outstanding U.S. Amateur Athlete Award. The keynote speaker was then-U.S. Attorney General Robert Kennedy. When Rafer gave his acceptance speech, he talked about his desire to help others and improve the lives of the less fortunate. Robert Kennedy was struck by the words Rafer Johnson spoke. After the awards presentation, the Attorney General invited Rafer to Washington, D.C. to meet President Kennedy and Sargent Shriver, the director of the new government agency, the Peace Corps.

The mission of the Peace Corps, to raise the standard of living in developing countries while promoting peace and understanding, dovetailed perfectly with Rafer's desire to help others improve their lives. In subsequent years, Rafer carried the message of peace and hope as a spokesperson for the Peace Corps to many people throughout the world.

In 1961, Eunice Kennedy Shriver began using her Timberlawn estate as a summer day camp for children with mental retardation in the Washington, D.C. area. Beginning the program as a weekend outing for the children, Eunice recruited high school and college students as counselors for Camp Shriver and her own children played along with everyone else. Eunice always felt that retarded children and adults had unfulfilled potential; Camp Shriver seemed to illuminate this potential and bring it to life.

Eunice and the counselors found that the children, when treated with warmth, were often friendlier. They also found natural artistic and athletic talents surfaced with tutoring and encouragement. Eunice realized that these qualities could lead to employment for teenagers and adults with mental retardation.

Eunice wanted more. During the first year of John Kennedy's administration, her efforts on behalf of people with mental retardation led to the appointment of a task force charged with devising legislation to address mental retardation. Eunice led the administration's efforts and helped to mediate panel disputes between two distinct factions. One faction sought to address mental retardation strictly as a genetic and prenatal problem; another favored education as a vehicle for improvement in the lives of the mentally retarded. She was instrumental in focusing the committee on a consensus resolution, then lobbied for the support of congressional leaders. In October 1962, the task force's report was presented to President Kennedy. Eventually more than 70 of its 112 recommendations were implemented.

Although the political leaders of the time were changing their attitudes toward people with mental retardation, Eunice saw that the public's attitude lagged behind. She believed that the most powerful message to capture the public's attention would be a personal revelation about her sister, Rosemary. After speaking with her father and mother, Eunice wrote a groundbreaking article which appeared in the September 1962 edition of the *Saturday Evening Post*.

In the article, titled "Hope For Retarded Children," Eunice wrote inspiringly, "Twenty years ago, when my sister entered an institution, it was most unusual for anyone to discuss this problem in terms of hope. But the weary fatalism of those days is no longer justified. The years of indifference and neglect are drawing to a close and the years of research, experiment, faithful study and sustained advance are upon us. To transform promise to reality, the mentally retarded must have champions of their cause, the more so because they are unable to provide their own."

Eunice ended the article with a quote from Dr. Maria Egg, a German psychologist. Egg wrote, "It is up to us to help extend respect for human dignity to those creatures also; it is up to us who live with them and who love them. For we know what they need and we know what they can give us...For these little flames radiate warmth and soothing quiet joy; they shine on the road that leads to the wisdom of the heart, to human maturity, and to true wealth."

From Eunice's efforts came stunning success—first, the creation of the President's Committee on Mental Retardation, then the introduction of landmark legislation, led by the Mental Retardation Facilities Act of 1963. This act paved the way for major changes to the Civil Service Regulations, enabling the government to hire thousands of men and women with mental retardation. The impact and interest sparked by this legislation prompted the establishment of the National Institute of Child Health and Human Development. It also influenced the founding of the Head Start Program by cultivating the importance of early childhood education.

Then, in late 1963, the Kennedy family and the nation shared the tragic loss of John F. Kennedy. The energy John F. Kennedy elicited from Americans, once bright with idealism, turned dark. As the violence in Vietnam escalated, so did violence in the streets of America. Rebellion at home was spreading beyond the Vietnam War. The youth of America were divided; while some dropped out of society altogether, others worked hard for change. The anthem of the youth movement became "Question Authority." Race riots broke out in Harlem and Watts while Ku Klux Klan members were shooting people in Selma. Assassination became a word invoked too often.

In 1964, Eunice Kennedy Shriver and her husband, Sargent Shriver, persuaded the Advertising Council to launch a major campaign to further educate the public about mental retardation. The Young and Rubicam advertising agency created billboard, newspaper and magazine ads for the campaign, as well as television and radio spots. The campaign lasted five years and used nearly 50 million dollars in free advertising time and space. Emphasis was placed on the fact that over 80 percent of people with mental retardation were capable of performing complex tasks and thus able to hold jobs in the community. In response to the ads, more than two million letters were sent to the President's Committee on Mental Retardation. Thousands of letters of inquiry poured in asking about information on volunteering opportunities and how to hire the mentally handicapped. Looking back, this campaign was the turning point in public education and awareness. It also further paved the way for the success of Special Olympics in America.

Eunice continued to operate the summer day camp at her Maryland home. Using her camp as a model, she recruited public and private organizations to create and administer similar camp programs in other communities. Between 1965 and 1968, more than 80 such programs were started. To further encourage physical fitness among individuals with mental retardation, the Kennedy Foundation joined forces with the American Alliance for Health, Physical Education and Recreation to create and promote a fitness awards program. These awards paralleled the President's Physical Fitness Awards—Gold, Silver and Champ Fitness.

Success in developing and promoting activities in physical fitness and recreation prompted the Kennedy Foundation to make a grant to the Chicago Park District. In 1965, the Chicago Park District piloted a program of activities and sports for people with mental retardation, utilizing city parks and recreation centers. The district decided that a citywide competition would attract the public's attention and increase the use of the facilities. District officials presented the idea to Eunice Kennedy Shriver at the Kennedy Foundation, and Eunice decided to enlarge the scope of the event. Working together, the Foundation and the district planned an international track-and-field meet scheduled for July 1968 at Chicago's Soldier Field. The event was to be called "Special Olympics."

Throughout the '60s, Rafer Johnson had maintained his commitment to his ideals. His friendship with the Kennedy family deepened. From 1961 onward, Rafer was aware of Eunice's efforts on behalf of people who were mentally disabled; within a few years, he helped advise the Foundation on athletic matters. Like a great many Americans, Rafer was heartened by Senator Robert Kennedy's declaration of his bid for the U.S. presidency. Rafer actively campaigned for Kennedy during 1968 and was at the candidate's side on the night of June 4th in Los Angeles when Robert Kennedy was gunned down.

The assassination of Robert Kennedy caused Rafer Johnson, and other Americans, to withdraw commitments and question the direction in which they perceived America heading. But in early July 1968, Eunice Kennedy Shriver called Rafer Johnson and invited him to participate in the first Special Olympics. Rafer's answer was a resounding "yes."

The inspiring growth of Special Olympics from 1968 to now is a testament to the indomitable spirit of challenged people and their supporters who hold firm to their dreams, despite adversity. Their compelling stories are on the pages that follow.

NEXT PAGE: An athlete holds dear his gold medal for one of the special events for athletes using wheelchairs.

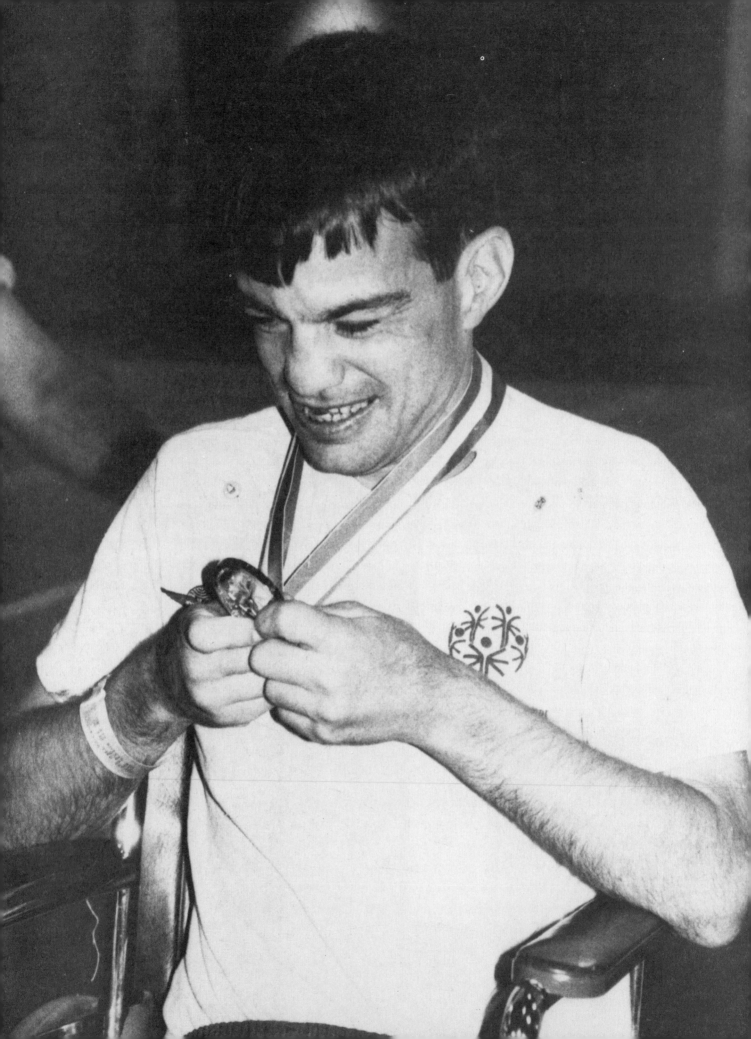

The Early Years—1968 into the '70s

1968

On July 19th, in 1968, one thousand athletes from 26 states and Canada traveled to Chicago. Each athlete checked into the La Salle Hotel and later enjoyed dinner, followed by entertainment: a magician and live music. The athletes danced with their new friends and fellow athletes. On July 20th, after breakfast, the athletes got on chartered school buses and were driven to Soldier Field for the Chicago Special Olympics. It was the beginning of a history-making day. Just a couple of years earlier, the idea of people with mental retardation getting together to compete in athletic events seemed incredible. Even in 1968, parents were still being counseled to place their developmentally disabled children into institutions and forget them.

But here they all were, the first one thousand Special Olympics athletes, marching in an opening parade, listening to Eunice Kennedy Shriver officially open the games, eager and ready to compete in track-and-field events, swimming and floor hockey. A new tradition, mirroring an old tradition, was instituted as the Special Olympics torch was run down the track and used to light the Olympic flame. One thousand balloons, each one bearing the name of an athlete, were released overhead, filling the sky.

Coaches, including the head coach, former Apollo 8 astronaut Captain James Lovell, were introduced one by one. Rafer Johnson proudly stood among the group of athletes. The Chicago Bulls turned out in force and put on a basketball clinic. The competition began and

OPPOSITE: The look of intense concentration for a softball throw shows the effort every athlete makes in developing his skills for competition.

new friends were made, leaving parents proud and surprised as a new world of success opened for the athletes. It was a day when everyone was a winner.

A film taken at Soldier Field that day shows children in shorts, slacks and bathing suits, running or swimming and having a great time. There are picnic tables set up in the middle of the field where snacks, beverages and lunch are served. The ambience and spirit of the day is somewhere between an extended family outing and a school event.

Training for the first Special Olympics was basic physical education, which included working out three times a week for thirty minutes. The basic workout consisted of: three minutes of warm-up (walking in place and stretching), five minutes of muscle-building (sit-ups and push-ups), ten minutes of skill-builders (running, long jumping, throwing, high jumping, basketball and swimming), five minutes of heart-builders (run-walk-run drills or fast-slow-fast swimming) and finishing with five minutes of warm-downs (walk-and-stretch or slow swimming).

With these first steps, everyone started running down the road to accomplishment, love and compassion—but most of all, to acceptance.

The following words of Rafer Johnson from the film *A Dream to Grow On,* about the Chicago Special Olympics in 1968, capture the spirit of the early organization most poignantly: "Winning an Olympic medal is the greatest thrill in sports. It's the dream of millions of school kids who work and train to run faster, swim faster, jump further or higher. I know it was my dream when I was a boy, and I was lucky there were teachers and coaches to help my dream come true. But you know, there

The 50-meter dash for athletes with visual impairment. The athletes guide themselves by sound and rope guides to complete the course.

are more than one million boys and girls in America who don't know what it means to dream of being a champion or making the team. Or being given the chance to run or swim or jump. They're the lonely kids you see walking silently along the streets of town, standing around watching while the others are playing. They're called mentally retarded. One-and-a-half million of them. They are three or four years behind in physical development because no one has helped them to catch up. No one has believed in them, so they don't believe in themselves. When they do try to join the fun, someone usually takes them by the

OPPOSITE: Twins compete at a local competition. Track-and-field events were some of the first sports offered by Special Olympics in the late '60s.

hand and leads them away. 'It's too rough,' they say. 'They might hurt themselves. They can't learn the rules.' But you know, when kids like this do get a chance, it's amazing what happens—brighter eyes, straighter, stronger bodies, keener minds. And they can dream of success, of winning a race, even of winning a medal."

While meeting the participants and accompanying them to receptions and small events, Rafer met a choral group comprised of children with mental retardation. The group was singing in front of Chicago's City Hall and were filmed with Rafer, which gave everyone a chance to talk and get to know one another. The director of the group told Rafer about the institution in Connecticut where they were

from and about its progressive program which encouraged the children in singing and other forms of creative expression. Rafer walked away that day knowing he could and would help the cause of people with mental retardation. He had met with and seen people who triumphed against the odds. Rafer knew a world of possibilities could be opened if he and others would lend a heart and a hand. He returned home to California with an enlarged sense of commitment.

In December 1968, Senator Ted Kennedy announced the establishment of Special Olympics Inc., created by the Joseph P. Kennedy, Jr. Foundation for the Benefit of Citizens With Mental Retardation. At this announcement, checks for $10,000 were presented to representatives of six U.S. cities which had plans to hold regional events. This was the start of a tremendous grassroots effort to take Special Olympics into every state and eventually into every country—a goal which is still being pursued.

1969

Richard Nixon was inaugurated as the 37th President of the United States at the beginning of the year. It was also the year that saw Sirhan Sirhan tried and convicted of the murder of Robert Kennedy, and James Earl Ray sentenced to prison for the assassination of Martin Luther King, Jr. The Vietnam War protests played as background to the trial of the Chicago Eight while *Oh! Calcutta* opened on Broadway and *Easy Rider, Midnight Cowboy* and *Butch Cassidy and the Sundance Kid* opened in theaters all over America.

The first Special Olympics training plan was

OPPOSITE: A special athlete waits for the official to fire the starting gun.

distributed. It was a six-panel brochure detailing the recommended thirty-minute, three-times-a-week exercise workout. The plan cautioned that athletes get a thorough physical examination by a doctor before beginning training and suggested, "If possible, several children should participate in the workout. Exercising with others makes the training more fun." Also included was an "athletes' dictionary" of 10 terms, one of which was "Special Olympics," which it defined as "a chance for you to win prizes for your physical fitness and skill in running, jumping, throwing, swimming and other sports." Listed on the back cover were Rafer Johnson as head coach, along with Suzy Chaffee, Dave Cowens, Donna De Varona, Wayne Embry, Carl Erskine, George Foreman, Rosie Grier, Don Meredith, Bill Toomey and Ed Westfall.

The organization's first regional event, the

The Special Olympics logo is made up of abstract humanistic forms designed to stimulate the imagination and convey the impression of movement, play and activity. The logo is impressionistic rather than realistic. The beholder can find in it whatever she or he wants to see: children dancing, exercising, throwing a ball. What is important is its identification with Special Olympics. It serves as a symbol of growth, confidence and joy—of special children and adults learning coordination, mastering skills, participating in competition and preparing themselves for richer, more productive lives.

The Olympic Connection

For Special Olympics athletes, the official recognition and association with the United States Olympic Committee (USOC) in 1971 and the International Olympic Committee (IOC) in 1988 has been a source of pride, automatically granting them membership into the world of athletes and the long history of athletic endeavor.

Exactly when the ancient Olympic Games started is unknown, but historians date the Games from at least 776 B.C. until 394 A.D., when the last recorded ancient Games were held. The games were held in Olympia, Greece because it was considered a religious, and therefore neutral, center where warring city-states could cast aside differences for competition. The Games were staged every four years for nearly 1,200 years. Their decline in popularity can be attributed to many causes, but their official end came in 394 A.D., when Emperor Theodosius forbade them, mainly because of their pagan origins. Natural disasters, war and the passing of time turned Olympia into ruins. It wasn't until 1829 that the first ruins of Olympia were excavated.

The first modern Olympic Games took place in 1896 in Athens, Greece and were the brainchild of Baron Pierre de Coubertin. Coubertin was inspired by the ancient Greek games, the excavated ruins of Olympia and the belief in the importance of sports as a ve-hicle for national self-esteem and the promotion of world peace. Coubertin wrote and lectured about the importance of physical education and proposed the restoration of the Olympic Games as an international event. He wrote, "Nothing in ancient history has given me more food for thought than Olympia, this dream city. Let us export our oarsmen, our runners, our fencers into other lands...and the day it is introduced into Europe, the cause of peace will have received a new and strong ally."

Finally, on June 23, 1894, the Congress of Paris voted unanimously to support the restoration of the Olympic Games and created the International Olympic Committee to control the development of the Games. Also restored were some of the ancient Olympic customs. "In the name of all the competitors, I promise that we shall take part in these Olympic Games, respecting and abiding by the rules which govern them, in the true spirit of sportsmanship, for the glory of sport and the honor of our teams," reads the oath of the modern Games, symbolic of the vow taken by the athletes of the ancient Games to follow the rules and be worthy of competing.

In the development of the Olympic Games, specialized sport experts organized their specific sport rules and codes of competition into international rules, and in the process, cre-ated individual sport federations. In the United States, the USOC is the sole coordinating organization for Olympic amateur sports. There are National Governing Bodies (NGBs) for each sport which work with the USOC to maintain the IOC guidelines.

Special Olympics, as part of the USOC and IOC, follows the guidelines set by the Olympic committees. The Official Special Olympics Sports Rules regulate the way all competition is conducted. The rules, based upon the sports rules of the International Sports Federations and National Governing Bodies for sports, were designed to protect the athletes and to provide fair and equitable conditions of competition. In all cases, the rules of these organizations are applied except for some standard Special Olympics modifications. One of the standard modifications is that Special Olympics competition divisions consist of a minimum of three and a maximum of eight competitors. Another is that all athletes who enter a Special Olympics competition receive an award recognizing their effort in the event; these awards designate the place of finish from first through eighth place.

In Special Olympics, everyone wins. The rules guarantee it.

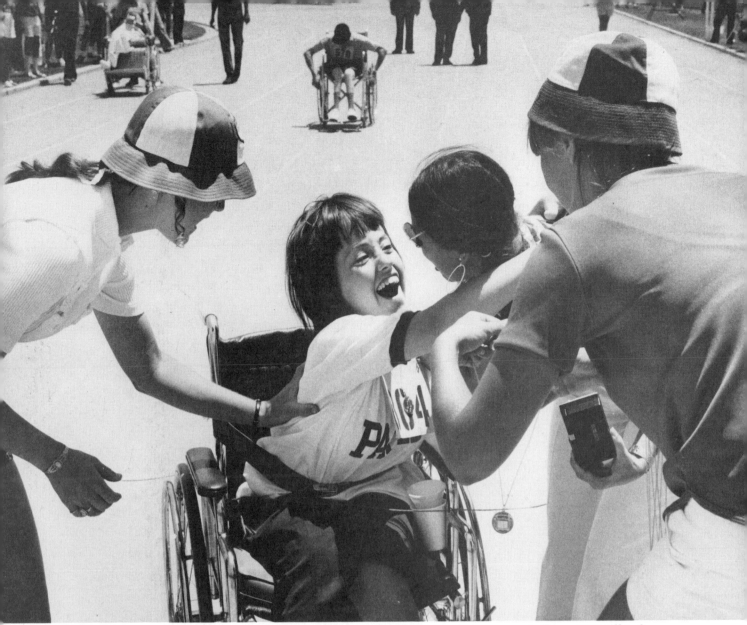

The joy of victory at the finish line...This is one of the very special moments in an event. From 1973 till today, the finish-line greeter is a coveted volunteer position.

First Annual Western Regional Special Olympics, was held on July 26, 1969 at the Los Angeles Memorial Coliseum. Athletes from Arizona, California, Colorado, Hawaii, New Mexico, Nevada and Utah participated in the softball throw, the 50- and 300-yard dash and the 25- and 50-yard swim. With the success of this event, each Western state began to formulate plans to organize its own chapter program.

1970

For Special Olympics, the first significant event outside the United States took place in France in June of 1970 as 550 young special athletes participated in the First French Special Olympics Games.

Meanwhile in America, the student confrontation at Kent State in Ohio made headline news and the Woodstock Festival in upstate New York ran for three days—both events helping to define a new generation.

While the youth movement was questioning the way society operates, parents and concerned persons were questioning the care, education and opportunities given to children and adults with mental retardation. Interest

in Special Olympics was growing. In fact, the 1970 International Special Olympics Games, held at Soldier Field in Chicago, doubled in size, from one thousand to two thousand athletes and included participants from four countries. Regional and state chapters were in the process of being formed.

1971

In February, an earthquake in Los Angeles caused one billion dollars in damage and killed 60 people, but planning for the 1971 Invitational Western Special Olympics continued. Athletes from Arizona, California and Oregon competed for the first time on the UCLA campus. That year's program included comments by G. Lawrence Rarick, Ph.D., Professor of Physical Education at UC Berkeley and developer of a standardized physical fitness test for moderately retarded children. Rarick reported the promising results of a recent study examining the effect of a physical fitness program on the behavior and attitudes of children with mental retardation. "Teachers, almost without exception, reported that the children who participated in the physical activity program were more highly motivated in the classroom," he wrote.

While research began to show the positive effects of Special Olympics, parents were discovering it themselves in the home. The psychological impact of success and acceptance on the sports field gave way to even greater successes. Parents noticed a marked difference in their children. Participating children demonstrated greater interaction with all

OPPOSITE: Two special athlete winners exchange excited words as one gives the "thumbs up" sign for a good performance.

members of the family, were in better moods at home, interacted with (and got along better with) a wider circle of friends and were generally better adjusted than before their Special Olympics experience.

The Kennedy Foundation provided a forum for the scientific community to pool research, sponsoring "Choices on Our Conscience: The First International Symposium on Human Rights, Retardation and Research." With science's growing ability to determine and control the nature of human life, and genetic engineering a reality rather than fantasy, the Kennedy Foundation was concerned about the ethics and social impact of scientific advancement. Abortion and fetus viability were hot topics of the day. Controversy raged around the value that society places upon citizens with disabilities such as mental retardation. A dramatic social revolution was underway.

The government also began to reevaluate its role in providing support to citizens with mental retardation. The President's Committee on Mental Retardation, chaired by Elliot L. Richardson, focused its attention on reexamining intelligence testing and classification procedures, states' systems for delivery of services to the mentally retarded, and the constitutional rights and guarantees of the mentally retarded. An outgrowth of these discussions was greater federal and state funding of developmental centers and sheltered homes for people with mental retardation. Institutions which had no unique care, no physical fitness program and no interaction were becoming dinosaurs.

In December 1971, the United States Olympic Committee gave Special Olympics their official approval to use the name "Olympics" in

Jan Sarnoff (second from the left) and a friend take time for a photo opportunity with Jack Benny and Jean Stapleton of Edith Bunker fame during the 1972 International Special Olympics Games.

its name. The use of the name "Olympics" means that Special Olympics seeks to uphold the spirit of sportsmanship and love of participation for their own sake. The Olympic creed is, "The most important thing in the Olympic Games is not to win but to take part, just as the most important thing in life is not the triumph but the struggle. The essential thing is not to have conquered but to have fought well." The Olympic motto is "Citius, Altius, Fortius;" the accepted translation is "Swifter, Higher, Stronger" and it represents the aspirations of all Olympic athletes. It's not difficult to

OPPOSITE: Athletes always appreciate the support and friendship of celebrities.

see how Special Olympics mirrors both the Olympic creed and motto.

1972

From June 22 to 25, 1972, in San Jose, California, the California State Special Olympics Games took place. Rafer Johnson, Special Olympics national head coach and a member of the state board of directors, was instrumental in assembling a roster of head coaches for 17 sports, including Mani Hernandez (U.S. Olympic Soccer Team, 1972) for soccer, Jim Turpin (U.S. Olympic finalist) for gymnastics, and others. Competition was held in track-and-field and swimming events.

Also in June, across the Atlantic Ocean in

Johnny Carson chats with Bob Newhart during a break in the Celebrity Hospitality Room. That's Dick Martin in the background.

France, world-champion skier Jean-Claude Killy, opened the Second French Special Olympics Games.

In August, the 1972 International Special Olympics, held at UCLA and Santa Monica City College, became the third nationwide Special Olympics event since Soldier Field in 1968. Participants numbered 2,500 and eight countries were in attendance. Rafer chaired and led the Area Coordinating Council for California. Tom Fitzsimmons served as vice

OPPOSITE: Susan St. James joins in to support Special Olympics in 1973. Celebrities will often be "assigned" a group of athletes to walk with during the opening ceremonies' parade of athletes.

president of training and games. The Los Angeles Rams team physician, John William Perry, M.D., joined the executive board as medical director.

Celebrity involvement helped bring the event to the public's attention. Mrs. Janyce Sarnoff, head of the special events committee, called on the actors from *The Mod Squad*—Michael Cole, Peggy Lipton, Clarence Williams III and Tige Andrews—who showed up in force. Arte Johnson, Ruth Buzzi and Lily Tomlin from *Rowan and Martin's Laugh-In* joined up with *Bonanza*'s Lorne Greene and Michael Landon. Special Olympics was beginning to catch America's eye.

A platform full of stars comprise the celebrity reviewing area for the 1973 opening ceremonies. See how many you can name.

The 1968 Chicago Special Olympics was a two-day event; in 1972, it took a full six days to fit everything in. Athletes and celebrity coaches taught sports clinics. Rosie Grier, Sue Gossick, Perry O'Brien and Patricia McCormick were just four of the more than 30 athlete-coaches who gave their time and skills for the athletes.

1973

Watergate dominated the news while Americans suffered through the Arab

OPPOSITE: Janet Leigh with Lorne Greene during the opening ceremonies at the 1973 Summer Games. You can also see Arte Johnson to the right, behind Janet.

oil embargo and gas shortages. For the first time, the name California Special Olympics appeared on a program alone. All of the states which started out as the Western Regional Special Olympics (Arizona, California, Colorado, Hawaii, New Mexico, Nevada and Utah) now had state chapters of their own, operated their own state games and bid on being selected as a site for future International Special Olympics.

The 1973 California Special Olympics State Games took place July 20th and 21st at UCLA. In the program, Eunice Kennedy Shriver answered the question, "Why is it called the Special Olympics?" She wrote, "All of us need to feel special. Mentally retarded children in

Two special athletes vie in the 50-meter dash during the 1973 Summer Games. In the background, you can see the stands filled with supporters. The special athletes really appreciate when people come out to wish them well.

particular face constant experiences of failure and frustration. Sport provides an ideal setting for developing confidence and a sense of self-esteem. The athlete trains, develops skills, competes and, as he succeeds, starts building a positive self-image. As a Special Olympics child improves his performance in the gymnasium and on the playing field, he also improves in the classroom, at home and eventually on the job. These children have always been told

OPPOSITE: George Peppard takes a coffee break in the Celebrity Hospitality Room during the summer games held in 1973. Celebrity attendance also helps ensure community involvement in coming out to watch the games.

they can't compete. They've been told they can't do it. But in Special Olympics we say they can do it. All they need is a chance. Special Olympics is that chance. Special Olympics involves the entire community with a group of children it had previously rejected. This involvement gives the Special Olympics participant and his family a sense of belonging. As a boy in California asked during a training session, 'You mean all these people are out here just to help us train? Do they really care about us?' Now the community can respond, 'Yes, we do care.' That is what is so special about the Special Olympics."

Rafer Johnson continued his work as spokes-

Hollywood Supports Special Olympics

Hollywood celebrities attend competitive events and present awards to the special athletes. Their participation is a thrill for the athletes, who love to collect autographs. Their visibility is appealing to the public and helps build attendance at the Games. Here's just a short list of star supporters:

Claude Akins • Marty Allen • Steve Allen • John Amos • Barbara Anderson • Richard Dean Anderson • Susan Anton • Bea Arthur • Billy Barty • Elizabeth Bauer •Jack Benny • Polly Bergen • Ted Bessell • Joey Bishop • Bill Bixby • Ray Bolger • Tom Bosley • Foster Brooks • Johnny Brown • Roscoe Lee Brown • Joyce Bulifant • Red Buttons • Susan Cabot • MacDonald Carey • Johnny Carson • Bernie Casey • David Cassidy • Michael Cole • Gary Collins • Mary Ann Mobley Collins • Mike Connors • Jackie Cooper • Bob Crane • Richard Crane • Richard Crenna • Bill Christopher • Linda Cristal • Billy Crystal • Jamie Lee Curtis • Cathy Lee Crosby • Pat Crowley • Robert Culp • Mac Davis • Sammy Davis, Jr. • Laraine Day • Danny DeVito • Kevin Dobson • Angie Dickinson • Janet DeBois • Barbara Eden • Geoff Edwards • Bill Eliott

• Leif Erickson • Dale Evans • Mike Farrell • Norman Fell • Robert Foxworth • Peggy Ann Garner • Cary Grant • Lorne Greene • Rosie Grier • The Hager Twins • Alan Hale • Monty Hall • David Hartman • June Haver • Hal Holbrook • Bob Hope • Susan Howard • Michael Jackson • Dennis James • David Jansen • Anne Jeffreys • Arte Johnson • Rafer Johnson • DeForest Kelly • Don Knotts • Harvey Korman • Yaphet Kotto • David Ladd • Diane Ladd • Fernando Lamas • Michael Landon • Walter Lantz • John Larroquette • Janet Leigh • Jack Lemmon • Jerry Lewis • George Lindsey • Art Linkletter • Peter Lupus • Paul Lynde • Bill Macy • Peter Marshall • Dean Martin • Dick Martin • Ross Martin • Ron Masak • Cathy Rigby Mason • Darren McGavin • Ed McMahon • Katherine MacGregor • Fred MacMurray • Bob Middleton • Marvin Miller • Don Mitchell • Elizabeth Montgomery • Mary Tyler Moore • Ben Murphy • Jan Murray • Bob Newhart • Leslie Nielson • Leonard Nimoy • Hugh O'Brian • Carroll O'Connor • Donald O'Connor • Nancy Olson • Norm Parker • George Peppard • Anthony Perkins • Jane Powell

• Carl Reiner • Rob Reiner • Lance Rentzel • Roy Rogers • Cesar Romero • Dan Rowan • Emma Samms • Dick Sargent • Arnold Schwarzenegger • Vince Scully • Martin Sheen • Dinah Shore • Mark Slade • Jaclyn Smith • Tom Snyder • Susan St. James • Robert Stack • Jean Stapleton • McLean Stevenson • Woody Strode • Susan Strasberg • Sally Struthers • Barry Sullivan • Bo Svenson • Loretta Swit • Joan Van Ark • Vincent Van Patten • Mitch Vogel • Robert Walden • Dionne Warwicke • Adam West • Billy Dee Williams • Maury Wills • Paul Winchell • Jonathan Winters

Eunice Kennedy Shriver with everyone's favorite comedian, Bob Newhart and his wife at a special event for Special Olympics.

person for Special Olympics International and for California Special Olympics. His schedule included fundraising, interviews and presentations to civic clubs, business meetings and conventions. In 1973, Rafer secured the single largest donation ever to California Special Olympics, bringing the organization out of debt and allowing for its continued growth.

1974

Jim Tunney, an educator and former NFL official for 30 years who is now a professional speaker, was asked by Jan Sarnoff to volunteer with California Special Olympics. When later asked to recall an outstanding moment, he said: "In every speech that I give, and I give about 75 to 100 a year, I always incorporate Special Olympics and I do it in the sense of 'what is it that motivates, what makes you want to do a better job, what stimulates you.' And what motivates me is June...in the month of June I have the great privilege to work in the California Special Olympics Summer Games at UCLA. And I've seen some incredible athletes. I saw an 11-year-old girl win the three-meter diving championship and she was blind. Now the next time you have a rough decision to make or the next time you question whether you have the courage to really *do* it, just think of the 11-year-old girl climbing up a ladder she can't see and can only feel. She takes twelve steps to reach the end of a board and she cups her hands, then dives into a pool of water that she doesn't see.

An athlete clears the bar in the high jump during the 1973 Summer Games.

She trusts the someone who only *told* her it was there. Courage, raw courage. Why would a girl who is blind take that kind of risk? Courage."

1975

Congress passed a law this year requiring that states provide a "free, appropriate education" for children who are handicapped. Special education programs were to be in place nationwide by 1978.

Early in the year, Mexican special athletes competed in a Special Olympics event in Nogales, Arizona for the first time. Mexico promised to send a delegation to the International Games to be held in August.

In a statement, Mrs. Shriver reflected on the greater acceptance people with mental retardation were finding in America in 1975: "This is a very special year for all Special Olympians. It's the year of the International Games and many of you will be trying to win a place on your state's delegation to Michigan in August. It's the year when ABC told the Special Olympics story to all America on its Barbra Streisand television special. It's the

Ethel Kennedy meets with special athletes in 1976.

year when 3,182 non-commissioned officers of the Non-Commissioned Officers Association ran from coast to coast to help raise funds for Special Olympics. It's the year that the National Basketball Association and the American Basketball Association sponsored our Special Olympics Basketball Team Tournament and Run, Dribble and Shoot Contest. And it's the year that CBS will cover the International Games live on television from Central Michigan University."

In August, the Mount Pleasant, Michigan, International Special Olympics Games hosted

4,000 athletes representing 17 countries. More sports events were added to the competitive schedule, including gymnastics, basketball, soccer, tennis and softball.

For the third year in a row, the name, California Special Olympics State Games, and the date, the third weekend in June, remained the same, setting the pattern for all future state summer games. The 1975 games took place at UCLA from June 20th through the 22nd.

Seven competitors start the 100-meter dash during the 1973 Summer Games track-and-field event. According to Special Olympics competition rules, no more than eight athletes may compete at one time.

1976

The United States celebrated its Bicentennial and Special Olympics celebrated having 500,000 athletes involved in its program in the United States and 12 other countries. "I can't think of a better place to celebrate the Bicentennial than right here at the 1976 Special Olympics Games. Everything that makes us truly American is to be found here. Courage. Generosity. Determination. And

OPPOSITE: Roy Rogers and Dale Evans were special guests for the 1977 Summer Games. All the athletes were thrilled to see their favorite western hero and heroine.

the spirit of volunteering with which Americans have always helped one another," wrote Mrs. Shriver in an open letter to Special Olympians, parents, volunteers and friends of the program.

1977

After years of social restlessness and with the United States out of Vietnam for two years, the focus of Americans turned optimistic. The first Concorde flight took passenger service from Washington, D.C. to Paris in four hours. The space shuttle *Enterprise* made its first manned flight. *Star Wars* and *Annie Hall*

Loretta Swit and a friend are greeted as they join the athletes on the field during the 1977 games.

showed the public's new fascination with outer space and inner space. Challenges—and conquering them—were personified by Cindy Nicholas, a Canadian who became the first woman to swim round-trip, nonstop across the English Channel.

Five countries sent 525 special athletes to Steamboat Springs, Colorado to participate in the First International Special Olympics

OPPOSITE: Michele Turnbull from Yolo County, California in front of the Olympic Village at Kirkwood.

Winter Games. Skiing and skating topped the program of new sports. For the first time, substantial support and funding was received from major American corporations. As at all Special Olympics and Olympic events, the opening ceremonies took place the evening before the first round of competition and started with a parade of the athletes. Teams, wearing uniforms designed in every color imaginable, entered the stadium greeted by the applause of their supporters. Next came the introduction of the guest professional

A close finish during the 1973 Summer Games 50-meter dash event. Uniforming in the early 1970s didn't follow professional athletics standards, but that was soon to change.

athletes who supported the athletes and conducted clinics. After the invocation was the raising of the American flag and the singing of the national anthem. Welcoming remarks were made by local dignitaries. Eunice Kennedy Shriver's welcome was followed by the raising of the Olympic flag and the recitation of the Special Olympic oath. The highlight, as always, was the torch parade which culminated in the lighting of the Olympic flame to signal the opening of the games. Fireworks, skydivers and a balloon release ended the

ceremonies and set the stage for the excitement of competition.

1978

Disco was "in" while Hollywood explored the impact of the Vietnam war on those who fought it with movies like *Coming Home* and *The Deer Hunter*. California Special Olympics was exploring the impact of training on special athletes. In February 1978, the Department of Health, Education and Welfare (HEW) awarded a three-year grant to the city of

Garden Grove, California for the institution of a general sport training program for people with mental retardation. The training sessions were scheduled to be held after school hours, during the summer and on weekends. The program proved so successful during the first year that it was used as a model for the first summer training camp for people with mental retardation in California. To provide proper training for the summer camps, California Special Olympics held the first coaches' training in Los Angeles.

In Chicago, Joe Bilder became the first special athlete to complete a city-sponsored marathon. Joe's finishing time in the Mayor Daley Marathon was just over four hours.

At Mammoth Lakes, the California Special Olympics Winter Games were held. Athletes from all around the state competed in alpine and cross-county skiing events.

With major corporations playing a larger role in funding of the games, policy needed to be set to avoid inadvertent conflicts or possible interference with the sponsorship relationship. Contracts needed to be signed to clarify everything from what type and size of signage was permitted to Special Olympics' approval of use of its logo.

Fundraising efforts did expand; however, it was not from the usual federal or United Way sources. Individuals, private and public corporations and community organizations played the major role in reaching funding goals. This remains true to the present.

1979

Now held every four years, by 1979 the International Special Olympics was a culmination of more than 17,000 local, area, chapter and national training programs and competitive meets in which nearly one million mentally retarded athletes took part throughout the world. The 1979 Games took place on the campus of State University of New York at Brockport. There were 3,500 participants from 20 countries. California was represented by a group of 90 athletes and 22 chaperones.

Mrs. Shriver opened the games by saying to all, "For great world athletes, the contest may last only minutes. Then it is over and they have won or lost. But for Special Olympians, the contest can last a lifetime. The challenge begins again each day. What they win by their courageous efforts is far greater than any game. They are winning life itself and in doing so, they give to others a most precious prize—faith in the unlimited possibilities of the human spirit."

California Special Olympics celebrated its tenth anniversary in March 1979. There were programs in 48 counties and 15,000 athletes participated in local training and competitive meets throughout the state.

By the decade's end, the Special Olympics program had more than 375,000 participants, 350,000 volunteers and chapters in each U.S. state and in almost 30 nations around the world.

Staging the State Games is a Volunteer Effort

In every state, there are Special Olympics chapters. Ninety nine percent of these chapters are volunteer-run organizations which raise funds locally to maintain and develop their programs. Support of the state chapters is embraced warmly by local corporations, associations and private persons. Committed volunteers number more than 65,000 and are comprised of teachers, coaches, family members and friends of Special Olympics.

Every Special Olympics chapter has annual state games. The work that goes into the staging of a competitive meet covers many months and includes many people—most of them volunteers. A venue must be selected which fulfills the NGB sport specifications, dates must be agreed upon and contracts drawn up, then signed. Practice and competition schedules have to be decided and must allow time for athletes who are participating in more than one event. Transportation must be arranged. A staffing plan must be compiled

and volunteers must be found to fill the positions, including: first-aid people, set-up and strike crews, athlete escorts, security and access control teams, drivers, volunteer check-in representatives, volunteer coordinators, hospitality-team representatives, runners, press/ media coordinators, judges, timing crews and more. Volunteers must be trained for their positions. Equipment must be obtained and delivery schedules set up for such things as tents, chairs, timers, awards stands, water coolers, water, batteries, tape, rope and so on. Signs need to be designed and produced for welcoming, directions, rest rooms and event locations. Medical and emergency procedures must be coordinated and communicated. And this is just a very brief overview of what it takes to run an event.

Volunteers play a very big part in making it happen. The California State Games have some 900 volunteers—mostly young people—involved in every phase of the three-day meet.

OPPOSITE: "Special Olympics is delightful because nobody is a failure. They are all successes," says Arte Johnson, shown here with Mike Farrell and Jan Sarnoff as they sign a Special Olympics poster.

Rafer Johnson

In 1944, Lewis and Alma Johnson brought their children Rafer, Jimmy, Eddie, Delores and Irma to the farming town of Kingsburg in the San Joaquin Valley of California. "I saw I had good boys growing up and everyone knows that California is the land of opportunity," Lewis Johnson told a *Sports Illustrated* reporter for the January 5, 1959 cover article on Rafer when he was named Sportsman of the Year. In the same article, Rafer said of his father, "He never pushed us in sports or anything, but he always wanted us to go farther than he had."

When Rafer was twelve years old, he had a horrible accident as he was climbing up a peach cannery conveyor belt. His left foot was torn open and mangled to such an extent that everyone thought it would need to be amputated—or that, in any event, Rafer would never walk again. The tear took 23 stitches and more than eight weeks to heal to a point where Rafer could go without crutches. The love and support of his family, teachers, friends and coaches helped him through this difficult time. Rafer not only walked again, but was soon hard at work in his high school's athletic program.

Continued hard work and talent combined with the interest and care given by Coach Murl Dodson and Rafer's teammates helped Rafer turn into a solid all-around athlete.

Even though later in his career other injuries were to occur, Rafer's ability to will his talents into action never faltered. The story of Rafer Johnson is filled with incredible athletic achievements.

Rafer Johnson's career is also filled with an amazing dedication to serving humanity. Even during his college years when sports training, competition and studying took up most of his time, Rafer rarely turned down requests to speak to or meet with groups. Always an inspiration to others, Rafer received and answered hundreds of letters from all over the world. Even today, Rafer personally responds to more than 1,000 people annually who write to him about Special Olympics.

In 1968, Rafer joined the board of directors of Special Olympics, Inc. Back in California, Rafer started calling on people to organize a Special Olympics on the West Coast and helped put together a Western Regional Special Olympics. His involvement with and enthusiasm for Special Olympics has been unflagging to this day.

Rafer Johnson Career Highlights

High School Achievements

- State high hurdles champion
- High school decathlon winner for two straight years
- Third place at the 1954 national AAU decathlon

College Achievements (UCLA , 1955-1959)

- West Coast relays, tied the U.S. freshman record
- Compton Invitational winner, fastest time worldwide
- Southern Pacific AAU decathlon, scored ninth on the all-time list and qualified for the Pan American Games
- 1955 Pan American Games, decathlon winner
- Central California AAU decathlon, highest scoring first day in history
- 1956 Olympic Games in Melbourne, Australia, silver medal winner
- Decathlon international winner against the new world record holder, Kuznetsov
- *Sports Illustrated* 1958 Sportsman of the Year
- 1960 Olympic Games in Rome, Italy, gold medal winner
- *Track and Field* 1960 Athlete of the Year

Ongoing Achievements

- The Sullivan Award, top amateur athletic Olympic award in the U.S.
- The Teddy Award, the National Collegiate Athletic Association's highest award
- California Special Olympics' Spirit of Friendship Award

Madeline Evans
Volunteer Area Director

Madeline Evans is a volunteer area director who has been with Special Olympics since the organization's beginnings in 1968. Initially, it was Rafer Johnson who got her involved. She recalls, "Rafer contacted a couple of people at our school and invited a group of people to present the program. Of course it started out very small. In Orange County, it started with only 200 athletes. Now, I'm up to 2,500. At that time, 1968, we only had track-and-field and swimming. Each year we progressed and Eunice would add on another sport to challenge the athletes to participate. We grew from those first two sports to 20 sporting events."

As a volunteer, Madeline worked through the schools, spreading the word about Special Olympics to one principal and one parent at a time. "Of course we had to do a lot of legwork, as you can imagine. We had to go to each school individually and present Special Olympics to them and show them the benefits of the program. And also to let them know there was a need, since so many of our children just sat home by the TV set and didn't move anywhere. The progress was phenomenal. As we grew, the children grew with us."

To this day, Madeline is involved with outreach, giving presentations to let educators know there is still a great need for the program. While Special

Olympics has made great strides, Madeline points out that there are still children with mental retardation who have never set foot out of the house and who have never gone anywhere overnight. These are the kids that Special Olympics must work twice as hard to reach.

Ten years before she began volunteering with Special Olympics, Madeline was already giving her time and compassion in working with mentally challenged children. In the 1950s, she heard about a schoolgirl who went to school with her son being "given" to a state facility for the mentally retarded. This prompted Madeline to ask if she

could care for her. The state arranged for Madeline to get a license as a care provider. By the time she was done, she had not only taken on caring for the original girl, but for three other girls from the facility as well. She remembers, "As the girls moved on, one got married and one moved back home because she just wasn't ready to go it alone. The other two were working. From then on, I started to take boys."

When Special Olympics came on the scene, Madeline used it as a springboard for encouraging the boys in her charge to become increasingly independent. "The boys, along with my son, went to every Special Olympics event available," she says. "And we did a lot of teaching—teaching them to become independent people, teaching them to have their own apartment. It was quite a challenge. The experience was quite emotional, but I learned a lot from them."

Madeline admits that emotion plays no small part in her involvement with Special Olympics—and she would have it no other way. She says, "You know, I still cry when the opening ceremonies start with the parade of athletes. I say when I stop crying, that's when it will be time for me to leave."

Kathy Mullen
Special Athlete, Gymnastics

Thirty-three-year-old Kathy Mullen has been involved with Special Olympics for 25 years. Kathy's mother, Carmie, was coaching a swimming program for children with mental retardation when someone mentioned to her that a new program called Special Olympics was forming.

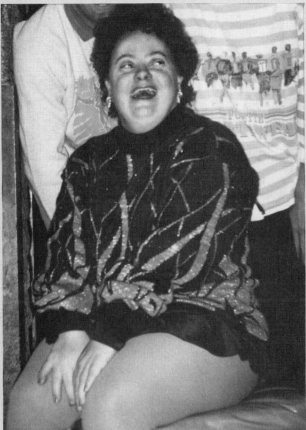

Kathy was eight years old when Carmie entered her into a Special Olympics swimming program. When she was just nine years old, Kathy made the newspapers in her home town of Fresno, California for winning a gold medal by taking first place in the 25-yard freestyle at the 1970 state games. Some of her biggest accomplishments in Special Olympics include being nominated for and winning the 1991 Spirit of Friendship Award for her outstanding performance at the 1991 Special Olympics International Summer Games.

With a history of outstanding performances, it will come as no surprise to learn that Kathy has won a place on more than four international games teams. Although Kathy started with swimming, she's now known for her gymnastics abilities. And Kathy's love of gymnastics is not just for competing—she also performs as a dancer with the Barrier Breakers Performing Team for Break the Barriers. Break the Barriers is a nonprofit organization integrating able and disabled people of all ages through sports and the performing arts.

Barrier Breakers Performing Team was started by Kathy's sister and brother-in-law, Deby and Steve Hergenrader, who have also been Special Olympics coaches for the past 25 years for gymnastics and powerlifting. As a Barrier Breaker, Kathy has performed at opening ceremonies for California Special Olympics for six years and also at the Sports Celebration Night for the International Special Olympics Winter Games.

Special Olympics is a Mullen family tradition. Kathy's father, Ken, who is now deceased, coached gymnastics. Carmie is still very active as a coach. Kathy's brother and sister-in-law, Jim and Judy Mullen, are also active volunteers. This kind of dedication and involvement resulted in the Mullen family being given the California Special Olympics' Outstanding Family Award and being nominated the Special Olympics International Outstanding Family during the 1991 International Games at Minneapolis. Kathy's accomplishments extend from Special Olympics into her community. She has received a volunteer award for her work as a teacher's aide at the St. Agnes Hospital Day Care Center and she has helped in fundraising events by modeling in several local charity fashion shows. Always on the go, Kathy loves a night out for dinner and movies with friends or bowling with her family.

As Carmie puts it, "Kathy is the Mikey of Special Olympics—she'll try any sport. She's determined, dedicated and filled with true team spirit."

Lisa G. Freedman
24 Years of Volunteering

Since she was 16 years old, Lisa Freedman has been a volunteer for the California Special Olympics Summer Games, held every June. Now 40 years old, Lisa recalls first learning of Special Olympics and her early volunteer years with the program: "My best friend, Lisa Gonzalez, heard about the program and said, 'Hey, why don't you come along with me and be a volunteer for Special Olympics.' I said, 'Special Olympics, what's that?' She said she wasn't really sure, but heard that it was for handicapped children. 'Just come,' she said.

"Well, I went and I was hooked," Lisa recalls. "The feeling was so overwhelming, the camaraderie and the love and people joining together to make a special weekend for these children. It was jam-packed with activities and celebrities. Johnny Carson, Buddy Hackett and Susan St. James came a number of times. For my first two years, I was an assistant at the celebrity photo booth and the funny thing was that there was a little nine-year-old girl helping me—and she turned out to be Jamie Lee Curtis. Her mom, Janet Leigh, would bring her along and she would take photos; she did that for many years."

Before long, Lisa was promoted to being an athlete escort. "They assigned me randomly to Marin County," she recalls. "I had never heard of Marin County, but I was more than happy to work with them. And then the following year, as a total coincidence, they assigned me to Marin County again. And so I said, that's it...Marin is *my* team. I've been with them ever since.

"The biggest joy over the years has been watching the athletes grow and change and develop," Lisa says. "I feel very close with many of the team members and especially look forward to seeing how they have progressed from year to year. I've even watched one boy grow up, get married and have a baby of his own. I've also developed friendships with the counselors from Marin and consider them as some of my closest, favorite friends."

Asked what she would tell prospective volunteers about Special Olympics, Lisa responds, "When you first start, you don't have a clue about how good it's going to be. Whenever anyone asks me, I tell them invariably that this is my favorite, favorite weekend of the year, without question. You totally forget about yourself and immerse yourself in the needs of others; you can just give and give. At the end, I always feel sad as the athletes are leaving. They get on their bus to go to the airport and it's a big, teary scene every time as you wave good-bye.

"I'm going to do this forever; I have no intention of stopping."

OPPOSITE: Lisa Freedman and Olympic gymnast Mitch Gaylord.

BELOW: Lisa marches with Marin County special athletes.

La Bryon Barton
Special Athlete, Track

When La Bryon Barton talks publicly, a friend noted, "he has very personal things to say. It's a moving experience." As an athlete in the outreach program, La Bryon travels and talks with civic groups and other organizations about mental retardation and Special Olympics.

"I first started in Special Olympics when I was twelve years old," he began a recent talk. "My mom had some problems. She sent me to school one day and said she did not want me anymore. Special Olympics makes me believe in myself. I went to Mission Bay High School and ran on the varsity track team and set a school record in the mile relay."

La Bryon grew up in foster homes, sometimes in rough neighborhoods. At school, one of his teachers who was also a Special Olympics coach introduced La Bryon to the program. Everyone agrees it changed his life.

Myra Snowdall, a friend and coach who has been involved with La Bryon since he lived in a foster home, says, "I remember going to the varsity track meets and seeing La Bryon's accomplishments in the regular arena. It was a real special moment for me. One of the best things about La Bryon is his gentleness with other athletes and his acceptance toward all the different disabilities."

When La Bryon turned 18 years old, he knew he had to find a different living arrangement. Today, La Bryon works at Longs Drugstore as a stock clerk and is proud to say: "I have my own apartment. I pay for my own bills and I do everything myself. In 1993, I was (Longs') Employee of the Quarter."

Kevin Reynolds, assistant manager and La Bryon's supervisor at Longs Drugstore, says, "La Bryon is one of the most dependable workers I have. He's always on time. He inspires other people through his positive attitude. He is always in a good mood and always does the best job he can."

"A lot of times people think of special athletes as very simple," says Jeff Washington, La Bryon's basketball coach. "But La Bryon is a very interesting guy, a very complicated guy. He worries a lot about things in the world. And he's a great athlete."

"It would be sad if I didn't have Special Olympics," La Bryon says. "Special Olympics has been my family since I was twelve years old. The coaches are like my father and mother. The athletes are like my brothers and sisters. Now I have a great big family."

Curtis Leslie Thompson
(September 29, 1949—November 6, 1974)

When Curtis Thompson was awarded the trophy symbolizing the Most Inspirational Athlete in the 1974 California Special Olympics State Games, his family and friends were never prouder. He had won a second-place silver medal in the 25-yard swim competition. Many other boys and girls won medals that day also, but for Curtis it was part of a dream come true.

At the time, Curtis had been stricken with cancer and had been advised by his doctors not to swim. His extended illness made it difficult for him to exert himself physically, but his spirit and his dreams supplied the impetus that eventually won his doctor's approval to enter the 1974 swimming competition. Winning the silver medal, he was the unanimous choice for the Most Inspirational Athlete Award.

In November, just five months after the state games, Curtis died. To the last, he shared his dream with his family. "Momma, I want to swim in the 1975 Olympics. I'm going to win that gold medal for you," he said repeatedly. For his spirit and perseverance, Curtis won something greater than a medal—he won our hearts.

Julie Wilsted
Special Athlete, Bowling

In her mid-60s, Julie Wilsted says she "loves to bowl and be with all the people." She has been involved with Special Olympics for seven years.

Pamela Moore, Julie's social worker, helps Julie on goal setting: "Julie is 64 years old and she has not slowed down at all. Her focus is on being productive. I think she views her work as an opportunity to show people that she is a human being and can do just about anything she wants to. She has a disability that will eventually make her less capable, but it hasn't slowed her down yet and she just keeps plugging along. She goes on, despite the fear, to attain her goal—and her goal is to live her life as independently as possible."

Julie lives in a residential group home and belongs to a work activity program at Hope Center where she packages products. Julie's supervisor at Hope Center says, "The most wonderful thing about Julie is that no matter what job she's working on, she just tries as hard as she can. Sometimes when she gets frustrated, she'll call me over and ask me to show her a different way to do something because she's having problems with the first way I've showed her. I'll show her another way and she always manages to do it."

Judy Kupfer, a rehabilitation therapist and Julie's bowling coach, remarks on her love of the game: "She's not the bowler

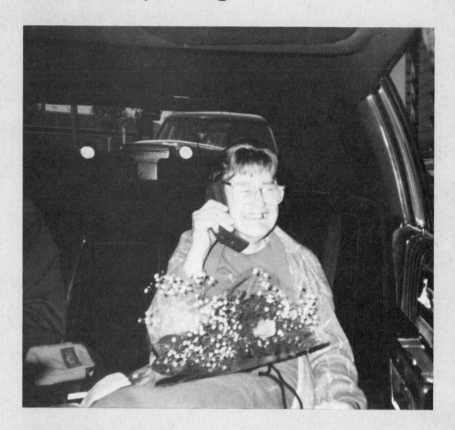

with the highest score, but I think her enjoyment of the game is most important and her social relations with other people are very important to her. When I met Julie, she didn't have a lot of confidence, but the activity and confidence you see today is all because of Special Olympics."

Another outgrowth of being involved with Special Olympics is Julie's work with People First, an advocacy group for people with disabilities. Gerald Curteman, an advisor for People First, had this to say about her: "She has shown me that she's a person beyond a disability. Julie brings her own persistence to issues.

She has a quiet strength where if you aren't willing to listen to her, she isn't going to force you to listen. She isn't going to raise her voice. She isn't going to push. But she is going to continue to pursue and find an ear until she feels her issues are heard."

When asked how she feels when she hears people say all these things about her, Julie responds: "It makes me feel happy and good. I like to help people."

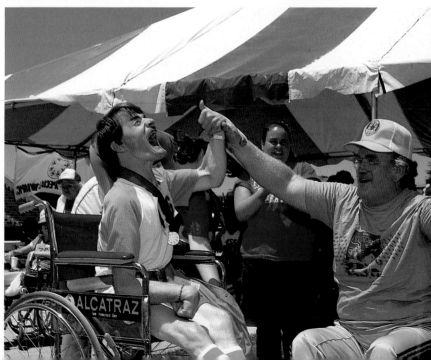

Joe Vasquez
Special Athlete, Track

Joe Vasquez got involved with Special Olympics in 1975 when he was 54 years old. He first trained and competed in the 50- and 100-meter run and the softball throw. Today, as a special athlete at age 73, Joe walks the 400-meter walk and participates in local area meets. He has even gone to state games to compete in this event.

Teresa Estrada, Joe's sister and only living relative, marvels at Joe's active social calendar, which not only includes Special Olympics, but also helping out at his residence and exploring the world of art. "Special Olympics has kept Joe in good health," Teresa says. "Years ago, my father passed away and Joe was placed in an institution. At that time, society was unkind. They didn't understand the problems of the retarded and so he was placed in a home for seven years. As far as I know, he didn't have much activity or much going for him. It was just a place to shut people away."

Today, Joe lives in a nursing care home for the developmentally disabled. Teresa recalls, "Four years ago, my brother suffered a heart attack and was taken to a hospital. I was called long distance by the doctors who asked me if I wanted them to discontinue life-saving procedures due to his other problems. I was quite upset by this and told them so. I also told them to keep him alive and I traveled to the hospital. To the surprise of the

doctors, he recovered completely. His quick recovery is probably directly related to his activity with Special Olympics."

After a complicated bypass surgery and extensive therapy, Joe once again took up his Special Olympics training schedule. Debbie Drum-Hall, Joe's coach since 1988, says, "Joe is incredibly inspirational. His quest for life is amazing. After his heart attack, he became a little depressed, but with the support of his Special Olympics friends, family and other individuals, Joe found the will to go on. Joe's life, for me and everyone who knows him, inspires us to live our lives to the fullest. Joe still walks every day and is signed up for the next area meet. He keeps an active social calendar and his health is good. Even at 73, Joe is as active as anyone at half his age."

Recently, Joe discovered he has a talent for art. The quality of his work attracted the attention of one of the local artists near his nursing home. She volunteered to teach Joe and he now takes regularly scheduled art classes with her. As a watercolorist, Joe has discovered a new way to communicate and has developed a great sense of pride about his work. Although many people have inquired about purchasing Joe's exquisite watercolors, they mean too much to him to let them go.

With Joe's health and activity level so high, plans are to move Joe from the nursing care home to a small group home. In the future, Joe has no intention of slowing down. His plans include painting more watercolors, continuing his art classes and competing in the next Special Olympics event.

Janet Tyler
Special Athlete, Ice Skating

At sixteen, Janet is a pretty, curly-headed brunette with a cheery disposition. She lives at home with her mother, Marianne Tyler, and her brother, Robbie. Janet has been involved with Special Olympics for nine years and is especially active in several winter sports, including ice skating and skiing.

"Janet was born totally normal," according to her mother Marianne. "She crawled and walked and ran. At about 15 months, I took her to the doctor for some little thing and that's when we discovered that she was having seizures. Well, she went from being a normal 15-month-old to a newborn baby again. She lost everything.

"When Janet was about seven, she decided she wanted to play soccer like her brother Robbie," Marianne recalls. "I went down, signed them both up and then, when I told them Janet was mentally retarded, they immediately gave me my money back and said that they couldn't accept her on the team. Well, she cried for at least a day. That's when I found out about Special Olympics."

Janet's ice skating coach is Janice Carroll. As in most special athlete and coach relationships, Janice says, "I think of Janet as a friend first. I know her on and off the ice and she's a really nice person to be around. Janet's also a real easy person to teach ice skating to because of her love for the sport."

Strong family support and a loving environment make it easier to cope with some of the rough spots for both Janet and Marianne. Janet's grandparents, Mr. and Mrs. Paul Bardsley, attend Special Olympics events locally and statewide. Janet's grandmother has noticed that "Janet loves everybody that she meets and everybody loves her." When asked what he would like for Janet, her grandfather says, "For Janet, my dream for her is to have a life that will be as satisfying for her as my life has been for me."

Marianne Tyler credits Special Olympics with helping Janet have a more fulfilling life. "At this point, Janet's capabilities are those of a five year old. It is at times difficult to have someone who is mentally handicapped, but there are a lot of pluses that make us feel lucky for what we have with her.

"Janet has memorized the Special Olympics oath—'Let me win, but if I cannot win, let me be brave in the attempt.' And each year I really see something better and better coming out of her. She's more outgoing, she's more confident and has so much self esteem. Well, where would Janet be if there wasn't a Special Olympics? I think it is wonderful that there's a program out there for these athletes who don't win scholarships to universities or real gold medals. The special athletes are just excited that someone cares."

Bill and Faye Munster
Special Olympics Family

The families of Special Olympians are special people. And Bill and Faye Munster of Southern California are very special. Bill and Faye have four boys—Bruce, Gary, Dale and Scott. Born in 1958, Dale has Down syndrome.

Children with mental retardation were invisible in 1958. Either they were institutionalized or they were kept "under wraps" in some other way. Bill remembers: "At that point in time there wasn't much available for

families. We got the same story from three or four doctors and you'll hear this story from just about everyone who had Down syndrome children at this time. All the doctors said Dale wouldn't be able to walk or talk and that his life expectancy was less than five years. So, they suggested we put him into a hospital and forget him. We didn't believe them and I know others who didn't believe them."

Bill and Faye were proud of their boys—all of their boys—and

Dale went everywhere his brothers went. In 1968, they read an article in their local newspaper about a committee starting to begin a Special Olympics program in their area. Dale was 10 years old when he began participating in the new program. Actually, it would be more accurate to say that the whole family participated in the program. While Dale was swimming, bowling, skiing and competing in basketball or gymnastics, Bill, Faye and the other children worked with both local and state Special Olympics programs to recruit additional families and athletes.

Dale participated in swimming, diving, basketball, floor hockey and gymnastics. It was in swimming and gymnastics that Dale won most of his gold, silver and bronze medals. For the International Games in Brockport, the Munster family drove cross-country from California to New York with 12 family members to cheerlead for Dale, who was competing. It was one of the highlights of the '70s for the whole family. Dale came home with a gold medal in gymnastics for floor exercise and a silver medal for tumbling.

The family involvement doesn't stop at recruiting and cheerleading—Dale's younger brother Scott, an outstanding high school and college basketball player, became a Special Olympics coach. Today, Scott works as a physical therapist to help those with even greater difficulties. Gary, another brother, is a physical therapist specializing in small handicapped children.

In 1982, Dale married his longtime girlfriend and fellow Special Olympics gymnast, Sandra. Since 1978, Dale has worked at various positions in the private sector. Today, at 37, Dale works for United Artists theaters and Sandra works for New Horizons as a maintenance person. Dale and Sandra also assist as gymnastics coaches in their home town of Reseda, California.

A third generation of Munsters has joined the ranks of volunteers—Scott's two young children now help at local meets and activities.

All the while, Bill and Faye are always present to lend a helping hand. They have this to say of the program: "Special Olympics is the greatest thing to come along for mentally challenged children and adults. It played a very large part in Dale's development. We want to thank everyone involved in this great program!"

ABOVE: Dale Munster performing his floor routine at the 1979 International meet.

OPPOSITE: Bill, Sandra, Faye and Dale Munster (left to right) together in Kona, Hawaii in 1992 to celebrate Dale and Sandra's tenth wedding anniversary.

NEXT PAGE: Maria Sanchez does her floor exercise routine in gymnastics at the 1987 Summer Games.

The Defining Years — 1980s

1980

Internationally, interest in Special Olympics grew rapidly. To meet the needs and requests of the many countries for help in developing training and competitive programs, a new Directorate of International Development was created.

Ronald Reagan became President of the U.S. and ushered in a new decade. Special Olympics ushered in a new decade with an emphasis on training. In the early 1970s, training programs were only "encouraged" year-round. Training was limited and without fixed standards. Although skill and fitness testing was introduced with the 1968 Chicago Special Olympics, it was not until 1979 that training programs for coaches were introduced.

Starting in the '80s, the training component was given new emphasis. Attention was focused on developing strategies for upgrading the quality of training as well as scheduling a greater number of training schools and coaches' clinics. The development of sports training camp programs became a priority. Sport rules and standards were starting to be set. Clinics were organized and qualified instructors were recruited. The North American Soccer League furnished players to conduct soccer clinics. More than 300 certified soccer coaches were recruited by the United States Soccer Federation to teach a 10-hour course to Special Olympics volunteer coaches. The head coaches associated with the National Basketball Association oversaw clinics for basketball coaches. A series of clinics were also scheduled by the National Hockey League.

OPPOSITE: Timmy Redmond gets ready to ride, but first a little brushing down for his special friend.

More and more, National Governing Bodies of sporting federations associated with the U.S. Olympic Committee became involved with Special Olympics. The '80s would be the decade of training improvement for Special Olympics.

"With the success of the 1979 International Summer Special Olympics Games behind us, the 1979-80 Special Olympics year has been one of intensified training in an expanded number of Official Sports. More training sessions have been held than ever before. Better training has been our goal," Eunice Kennedy Shriver wrote to the parents, athletes, coaches, volunteers and friends of Special Olympics in 1980.

1981

Smugglers Notch and Stowe, Vermont were the host cities for more than 700 athletes from 11 countries for the International Special Olympics Winter Games. Athletes competed in a full range of winter sports. Since the first winter competition was held in 1977, Special Olympics had been encouraging the training and coaching of winter events such as ice skating and skiing. By 1980, nearly all athletes within the U.S. and international chapters were participating in winter sports. All athletes were beginning to participate *year-round*. In Smugglers Notch, the athletes used a preexisting race course for their competitions. For the first time, a 1K cross-country skiing race was added to the events. Turner Broadcasting, with JoJo Starbuck as commentator, televised coverage of figure skating and speed skating events.

In Vermont, the competitive program was more diverse than ever before, including

Girls' soccer competition at the 1983 Summer Games competition.

summer sports which could be played either inside or outside—basketball, swimming, track-and-field and volleyball—and winter sports which could be played either inside or outside—ice skating, figure skating, cross-country and downhill skiing.

1982

The year opened with Ricky Wittman, a special athlete from Burbank, California, starring in *The Kid From Nowhere,* a television movie about a Special Olympics family.

OPPOSITE: Brett Honig starts his downhill run at Echo Summit during the 1985 Winter Games.

Neoli Fairhall won the gold medal for archery at the 12th Commonwealth Games and became the first paraplegic to achieve medal status in athletic competition. Special Olympics continued to grow, both in the number of events sponsored and the number of special athletes and volunteers participating. By 1982, one million athletes would compete in 19,000 local games, 900 area games and 250 chapter events with more than 325,000 volunteers taking part.

The year also saw California Special Olympics launch a commitment to offer regularly scheduled competition and certified training

Jenny Skinner rides Foxy, one of her favorite mounts, during an American Riding Club for the Handicapped event.

for coaches. To meet these objectives, recruitment efforts to find a full-time Sports Director were launched. By March, the first 25 coaches in track-and-field had been certified.

1983

The 1983 International Summer Special Olympics Games had 4,300 participants from 50 countries competing at Louisiana State University in Baton Rouge. Befitting Special Olympic's 15th anniversary, the Games provided the occasion for many events

OPPOSITE: John Dransfield proudly wears his gold medal from the 1983 International Summer Special Olympics Games held in Baton Rouge. International games give athletes a chance to meet and make friends from other countries.

such as the Presidential Premiere of *Superman III* in Washington, D.C., which benefited Special Olympics, and a 90-minute ABC special on the International Games. An astonishing 65,000 people were in the stands for opening ceremonies.

"In every way, the 1983 International Summer Special Olympics Games represented a benchmark of excellence toward which every Special Olympics organization should aspire," wrote Mrs. Shriver. "They were a measure of how far we have come since 1968 and a challenge to excellence in the years to come. The 1983 International Games were significant for many reasons. They affirmed the value of quality sport training and competition at every

Opening Ceremonies

The torch is lit. Let the games begin! Opening ceremonies commence yet another Special Olympics International Games.

In a darkened stadium, large spotlights move over the field, as thousands of people sit waiting for the parade of athletes to begin. Athletes from all around the world march into the stadium, carrying the banner with their program name emblazoned in colorful designs. The cheering audience stands up to applaud and shout their welcome. The athletes beam, their smiles seemingly brighter than the spotlights as they wave back.

Walking proudly, confidently, they march in, one group after another. Their uniforms are every color of the rainbow and so are their faces. They are men and women, boys and girls. Parents have tears in their eyes as they see their son or daughter entering the stadium. After they march in, the athletes take their places in the stands and stand up to cheer and wave their fellow athletes into the stadium.

As the night grows darker, the cheers grow louder and the excitement builds. Then silence falls as the program begins. Community religious leaders offer invocations. Everyone stands for the Pledge of Allegiance and the singing of the National Anthem. The applause and cheering begin again when Rafer Johnson officially welcomes all of the athletes. And just as the welcome finishes, the night sky is filled with dozens of brightly colored lights, leaving trails of pink and purple smoke. The lights come closer to the earth and the audience sees they are carried by skydivers, their parachutes wide open. The skydivers land as their flares die out.

Music starts to fill the air as special gymnastics performers demonstrate rolling and tumbling. Afterwards, all stand as the athletes recite the Special Olympics oath. The words carry on the winds and across the campus into the city streets.

Another light, a single, solo flame of hope, comes into the stadium. The runner carries this torch, a symbol of the Olympics, and lights the flame which will burn until the games are pronounced over. With the Olympic flame burning bright, fireworks light the sky and doves are released and fly upward.

An athlete performs a balance beam routine as her coach looks on. Coaches donate their time and give invaluable support to athletes in training.

level, giving athletes confidence and self-esteem, which, together with skill, are the true gifts bestowed by Special Olympics."

One of the special athletes who competed at Baton Rouge is Raymond Snyder from San Francisco. Raymond is a wheelchair special athlete with severe mental retardation. Raymond has no legs, but his talent for gymnastics won him a place on Team California for the International Special Olympics Summer Games. During the Games, Raymond competed, but found himself being disqualified from one event after another. The gymnastic rules called for "standing" positions in the compulsory routines and Raymond was physically incapable of standing. But Raymond persisted and remained "brave in the attempt."

Raymond competed in all his scheduled events and his enthusiasm never wavered, even though he didn't receive any medals. At the end of the competition, Raymond impressed his coach and his supporters with his spirit. They got together and had an award created and presented to Raymond—Most

The Step-by-Step Process an Athlete Takes to Compete in the International Special Olympics Games

1. The first step a prospective Special Olympics athlete should take is to call or visit the state or local Special Olympics office or program nearest his or her home. Since Special Olympics is free, there is no cost for participation or registration. Interested persons under the age of eight may participate in the training program, but they will have to wait until they reach their eighth birthday to begin competing.

2. As with any sports or fitness program, Special Olympics requires that a brief medical history and physical examination be completed prior to engaging in training. Often, doctors and medical practitioners will provide these physical examinations as a public service to future Special Olympics athletes.

3. Once registered, an athlete is given an opportunity to select from the many sports offered by Special Olympics. These choices are often limited by the location and scope of the program. However, it is important that the athlete choose a sport that he or she likes, and one that best fits his or her needs at the time. Coaches and parents can play a role in assisting the athlete with the decision.

At times, parents, coaches and even well-intentioned volunteers and professionals can become obstacles to an athlete's participation when they are too quick to say, "No, you can't do that." More often

than not, the athlete can and does succeed in the chosen sport. Special athletes may consider any sport and receive instruction in any number of events until they discover the ones most comfortable for them.

4. During the eight-week training process, coaches play a significant role in developing the athlete's talents, no matter which event is chosen—even if it is not the most obvious or generally acceptable choice. As athletes progress in their training, their coaches keep track of their times and distances, measuring their success as the training period continues.

5. Scores gathered during training are used for placing athletes into competitive divisions. Special Olympics divisions are structured to allow athletes to compete against other athletes of similar age, sex and ability. The ability factor is the most important principle in Special Olympics competitions—each division should have no more than a 10-percent variation within its competitors' abilities. These divisions, comprised of between three and eight competitors, allow every person a reasonable opportunity for victory.

6. Once the competition phase of the sport season begins, athletes advance to greater levels of competition, from the local level in their home towns to the area or county level of

competition, then onward to statewide competition. Each time, athletes are again placed in the divisions according to their abilities.

7. Every four years, athletes are selected for world competition. Because of the sheer numbers of participants, only athletes earning gold medals at their statewide competition are eligible for the few allotted positions on their state's World Games team. Gold medal winners are selected from a random draw to fill each of the team positions in the individual and team events offered at the World Games. At the Special Olympics World Games, the divisions are created using the same criteria that each state chapter uses, only this time, athletes may be from one of over 120 countries who have also earned the right to represent their state or country in competition.

This ongoing progression of sports training and competition provides a great incentive for athletes to work hard and to compete. The process restarts every year, providing athletes the opportunity for ongoing, lifelong participation in the Special Olympics program.

Inspirational Athlete. And the rules of the gymnastic competition have been changed.

In California, a research study conducted at a sports camp produced important results. The sports camp provided intensive sport-specific training for special athletes. Before attending the sports camp, athletes were tested to determine their pre-training skill development. During the training, athletes were tested for skill development improvement halfway through and at the end of the training. No other training was scheduled for the special athletes. Follow-up tests were scheduled and conducted at three-month, six-month and nine-month increments.

The study showed that while significant improvement occurred due to the sports camp training, sport skills diminished over time when training refresher sessions were not given to the special athlete. Demonstrating that ongoing training greatly improved special athletes' performances, this study helped support Special Olympics' emphasis on and funding of continued training programs.

In 1984, the Summer Olympic Games were scheduled to be held in Los Angeles. California Special Olympics moved the location of its Summer Games from UCLA to the University of California, Berkeley, as the UCLA venue was being prepared for the Olympics.

1983 saw more than one million athletes, 450,000 volunteers and 60 nations participate in Special Olympics International. While the organization's efforts were concentrated on training coaches in the early '80s, in 1983 Special Olympics International announced the establishment of their official training program for athletes. Before long, this program was implemented in all chapter programs.

Olympians and Special Olympians

Olympic athletes teach at Special Olympics training camps, attend competitions, award medals, act as head coaches and help in fundraising efforts. The list of Olympians who have been involved with Special Olympics is impressive. Here are just some of them:

Evelyne Hall Adams, Tai Babilonia, Brian Boitano, Dick Button, Milt Campbell, John Carlos, Jennifer Chandler, Bart Connors, Donna de Varona, Keith Erickson, Randy Gardner, Francis Gorman, Dorothy Hamill, Bruce Jenner, Jackie Joyner-Kersee, Jean-Claude Killy, Dr. Sammy Lee, Greg Louganis, Bob Mathias, Pat McCormick, Julianne McNamara, John Nabor, Mary Lou Retton, Mack Robinson, Murray Rose, Bob Seagren, JoJo Starbuck, Dwight Stones and Bill Toomey.

1984

On March 24, when President Ronald Reagan awarded Mrs. Shriver the Presidential Medal of Freedom, the nation's highest civilian honor, his words were eloquent and illustrative of the effect one woman made and continues to make. "With enormous conviction and unrelenting effort, Eunice Kennedy Shriver has labored on behalf of America's least powerful people, the mentally retarded. Over the last two decades, she has been at the forefront of numerous initiatives on behalf of the mentally retarded, from creating day camps, to establishing a research center, to the founding of the Special Olympics program. Her decency and goodness have touched the lives of many, and Eunice Kennedy Shriver deserves America's praise, gratitude and love." To say that Mrs. Shriver almost single-handedly changed the way an entire world viewed

The '84 Olympic Games mascot, Sam, joins Fran Spears, Rafer Johnson, Governor George Deukmeijian, Arte Johnson and a special athlete at the State Capitol Building in Sacramento, California.

people with mental retardation would not be far from the mark. Over the course of her life thus far, her dream of bringing the mentally retarded into the mainstream of society has been realized slowly. She is personally responsible for immeasurably enriching the lives of those with mental retardation by bringing them into full participation in communities,

OPPOSITE: Basketball during the 1984 Special Olympics Games held in Berkeley. You can see both concentration and fun in the players' faces as the ball goes up to score a point.

schools and workplaces. Special Olympics was a precursor to the larger disabled rights movement and was often used as its model.

From July 28th to August 12th, the Games of the XXIIIrd Olympiad were held in Los Angeles. Heading the Los Angeles Olympic Organizing Committee was Peter V. Ueberroth, a businessman who tried out for the U.S. Olympic water polo team in 1956, as well as a Special Olympics supporter. Ueberroth honored everyone in Special Olympics when he dedicated the last day of the Olympic torch run

Volunteers Keep It Happening

A volunteer gives a little last-minute advice at the starting line during the 1983 Summer Games.

"I'll never forget my first experience as a Special Olympics volunteer. I don't know who was cheering louder, the athletes or me."
—Jonathan Payne, Volunteer

Special Olympics is run almost entirely by volunteers. In California alone, more than 30,000 dedicated people give thousands of hours each year as area directors, chaperones and support volunteers.

And volunteering doesn't stop once you step off the playing field. There are volunteers who help with the administrative side of the organization—from helping to stuff envelopes to typing letters and making calls. Members of the board of directors are all volunteers, as are the coaches. Businesses and individuals work with Special Olympics to plan fundraising events to benefit the program.

And just about everyone who volunteers feels the same way that corporate attorney Frank Cooke does: "I could never give back to Special Olympics what it has given to me—the joy and satisfaction in working with the athletes is immeasurable."

1985 Summer Games medal winners show their gold to Olympic gold-medalist Rafer Johnson. Rafer's involvement with Special Olympics dates back to the beginning of the organization.

relay and 10 kilometers, or 10 legs since each leg was one kilometer, to California Special Olympics. More than $100,000 was raised that day for California Special Olympics.

"During the 1984 Olympic Games in Los Angeles, Special Olympics was far from forgotten," Mrs. Shriver said. "All over America, Special Olympics took part in the thrill of the Torch Relay and the public responded with enthusiasm and generosity. Our own head coach, Rafer Johnson, carried the torch to its final destination and many great Olympians, past and present, spoke proudly of their role as coaches in Special Olympics."

To commemorate the Olympic Games and Special Olympics connection, California Special Olympics held a Spirit of Friendship Award Dinner in the fall of '84. At the dinner, Olympians who have promoted Special Olympics were honored and presented awards for their valuable contribution.

1985

The International Winter Special Olympics Games were held in Salt Lake City and Park City, Utah, with nine hundred athletes from 14 countries attending. Dublin, Ireland hosted the first European Special Olympics Games. The Games started with colorful and spectacular opening ceremonies. The Irish

As this gymnast can tell you, there's no feeling that compares to winning a gold medal.

spirit showed through with children dressed in traditional garb and regional costumes. Athletes from the United Kingdom competed with athletes from Ireland, France and Germany. National differences paled against the depth of caring and joy that these games generated.

"The idea of Special Olympics, its belief in the abilities of mentally retarded people, its confidence in their families and its faith in the dedication of volunteers, has spread to many

OPPOSITE: After winning a medal in an equestrian event, this special athlete is riding high.

more nations of the world," Mrs. Shriver wrote of the growing international impact of Special Olympics. "The People's Republic of China sent observers to the International Winter Games. Bolivia, Panama and New Zealand held their first National Games. Special Olympics' flame of hope burns brightly in more than 60 nations."

Eight new countries—Tunisia, Monaco, Switzerland, Austria, The People's Republic of China, Gibraltar, Portugal and Yugoslavia—joined Special Olympics. New Zealand, Yugoslavia, Korea, Panama and Bolivia staged National Games for the first time ever. In

Educating Our High School Students

A high school coach can be the ideal link between special athletes and their high school communities. Since high school athletic coaches must be certified by the National Governing Bodies of their sports, they are essentially pre-certified to train for Special Olympics.

Coaches can arrange for the use of the school facilities for practice and can recruit the high school team to help train the athletes, which provides two important benefits: first, the athletes are given the chance to interact in a training and social situation with the community; and second, the high school students are introduced to Special Olympics and the athletes. Such exposure can go a long way in combatting high school students' discomfort with and prejudices against their peers with mental retardation.

Bill Fields, Director of Training for California Special Olympics, often participates on the last day of a basketball camp for high school seniors to introduce Special Olympics to them. Describing his approach to educating the high schoolers he meets, he says: "I ask how many of them have heard of Special Olympics. Many have. Then I ask them, 'How many of you have called someone retarded?' And usually just about all of them raise their hands.

"Then I say, 'But you call them retarded because you're trying to call them stupid, isn't that right, and there's a difference. Retardation is a disability. It's like somebody that has cerebral palsy. It's like someone that has one eye. Retardation doesn't mean anything derogatory, so don't call your friends retarded when you mean they're acting stupid. Let's look at the words now. Retardation is a disability— being stupid is by choice. When your parents ask you to take out the garbage once, twice, three times and they let you know that you'll be grounded if the garbage doesn't go out on the fourth time and you still don't take out the garbage and you get grounded — that's stupid.'

"Then I take it down another road. I ask them, 'How many of you laugh at the special education students in your school?' A lot of them raise their hands. I then ask them, 'How many think the reason they're in special education classes is because they're stupid?' The hands go up again. I say, 'No, they are in special education because they learn slower than you do, not because they are stupid. There's a difference. They may be slow, but they are not stupid. They may have other handicaps, but a handicap does not mean someone is stupid.'

"Now, this is probably the first time anyone has ever sat down to have a frank discussion with these high school students about mental retardation," Fields points out. "Many of these students will stop using the word retarded as an insult. Continued interaction (with special athletes) will help to eventually evaporate the negative connotations which often, unfortunately, continue."

U.S. Water Polo Olympian Terry Schroder comes out to support special athletes. He is shown here with a fan during a 1987 Winter Games competition.

Bolivia, 30,000 people came to watch and applaud the athletes.

The following quote from Mrs. Shriver, given as the opening address at a conference, is a hallmark statement on the program. "Special Olympics is a program involving mentally retarded people of every age and every level of ability. But it is not *for* the mentally retarded, it is *with* them. We believe in the principle of sharing our lives together. All of us. At every level from the family to the nation. We are a program of volunteerism—of support freely given by corporations, community leaders, teachers, religious leaders, students, profes-

sionals and parents. Special Olympics believes in a world that inspires excellence in the mentally retarded and ourselves. We demand the highest quality of training, of competition, of facilities and equipment. We believe that the spirit of Special Olympics transcends race, religion, age, national boundaries, mental handicaps and political philosophies. In our sharing with the mentally retarded, all are welcome; none are excluded. All are valued; none are disdained. This is our dream—that Special Olympics can be a catalyst to unite the world. Through Special Olympics, the mentally retarded have brought the citizens of the world

together in a universal celebration of skill, courage, sharing and joy."

1986

By 1986, training had taken a major leap forward. Bill Fields, director of training for California Special Olympics, offers his personal view of how Special Olympics training evolved. "I've been involved with Special Olympics for a total of 13 years now, five of those first years with New Jersey Special Olympics. In the '70s, training was just a basic physical education program. If we could get the athletes out to the track and run it straight, then the coaches felt their job was done. If you could run, you were running in the 100-meter dash. And that was that. And if you had a good arm, you were throwing the softball.

"You cannot expect an athlete to properly perform in street shoes and tight jeans, yet that's what they were doing in the '70s," Fields continues. "Today, we get our athletes into a uniform and into proper running shoes. The change came about because as Special Olympics started to grow and as more events were added, we needed the technical advice of (experts from) each and every individual sport. Special Olympics receives the information from the United States Olympic Committee that will maximize the performance of each of the athletes they work with. This is the same information that the Olympic athletes receive. That's how it is today, that's why we're proud to say that we work our program under the

OPPOSITE: A wonderful performance on the rings gets good scores. One of the special athlete's best friends is his coach—on the rings and off.

auspices of the United States Olympic Committee."

For the first time, powerlifting was introduced as an official competitive event. The new sport's importance soon became obvious as everyone observed that participating special athletes took on the form and appearance of weightlifters. Special athletes embraced, were welcomed into and quickly assimilated the unique culture of weightlifting. Consequently, powerlifting has turned out to be one of the most normalizing, mainstreaming events in the Special Olympics program.

1987

When Greg Lemond of Sacramento, California became the first American cyclist to win the Tour de France, it inspired "The Ride Across America." Led by volunteer Jim Benson, "The Ride Across America" took as its theme "Ordinary people doing extraordinary things," as 23 special athletes and 18 coaches from California Special Olympics rode their bicycles 2,600 miles across America from Newport Beach, California to Jacksonville Beach, Florida to raise awareness of Special Olympics.

The 1987 International Special Olympics Summer Games were held in South Bend, Indiana at Notre Dame University and St. Mary's College. The largest games ever, 4,700 athletes from 73 countries traveled to compete there. Paul Hoffman, a special athlete with Team California was selected to present a gift to then-Vice President George Bush, a guest at the opening ceremonies. All members of Team California were adopted by the Norte Dame Alumni and Studebaker Club during the games. One night, Team California was taken out to dinner in style—the special athletes

The 4x100-meter relay team from East San Gabriel Valley give the "We're number one" sign after competing.

were driven to the restaurant in vintage Studebakers. With more than 60,000 people in attendance and ABC airing the events to more than 10 million viewers worldwide, these games had the largest Special Olympics audience ever. For the millions watching, there could be no doubt about the courage and abilities of mentally retarded people and the strengths of their families.

The first *Very Special Christmas* album was released, with proceeds benefiting Special

OPPOSITE: A medalist flashes that familiar award-winning smile and the triumphant gesture of victory.

Olympics. The album was a project that rock producer Jimmy Iovine, who had worked with Bruce Springsteen, U2 and the Pretenders, had been wanting to put together for a long time. His wife, Vicki, an attorney who volunteers for Special Olympics in California, helped organize the project. Jimmy enlisted the support of A&M Records and then rounded up 15 recording artists. Vicki and fellow coordinating producers, Bobby Shriver and Paul Marshall, worked at securing free studio time, obtaining waivers from the musicians' union and reaching agreements with artists, their

Living Arrangements for People with Mental Retardation

There are four medical levels of mental retardation—mild, moderate, severe and profound—and this is ultimately a factor in the choice of residential setting for a person with mental retardation. A recent study showed that five percent of adults who are mildly handicapped live independently, some owning their own homes.

Nearly 60 percent of mentally handicapped people live in their family home, regardless of their handicap level. Living at home offers the advantages of a loving, supportive environment with parents, siblings and close family friends at hand, allowing for a greater chance of social interaction with a wider range of people.

If school-aged, they may be attending special education classes in community schools. If adults, they may hold jobs in fast-food restaurants, grocery stores or any number of places where they can perform the work.

Twenty-three percent of the people who live in community care facilities are mildly or moderately handicapped. Community care facilities are group living settings where a support staff cares for residents. Most likely, the residents attend school and other special programs or hold jobs and interact socially with their community.

Of the eight percent of the handicapped living in developmental centers, more than half are profoundly handicapped. People who live in developmental centers may have two or more developmental disabilities, as well as other medical or behavioral problems, such as sight or hearing loss. The care offered at these facilities is intensive and varies according to the unique needs of the individual.

management and record labels. A&M's art department designed the package, including an original drawing donated by artist Keith Haring for the album cover. The artists who donated their talent free of charge to the album were Bruce Springsteen, Whitney Houston, Madonna, Sting, John Mellencamp, U2, Stevie Nicks, Bob Seger, the Pointer Sisters, the Eurythmics, the Pretenders, RUN-D.M.C., Bryan Adams, Bon Jovi and Alison Moyet. By 1992, sales from the record had raised $17 million for Special Olympics.

1988

A growing number of women athletes became involved in the program in the late '80s. Girls and women with mental retardation discovered equal enjoyment and benefits in sport activity and competition. The status of women is best symbolized by Loretta Claiborne, a special athlete from Pennsylvania with 24 marathons under her belt and a personal best time of three hours and nine minutes.

"When I was in school, I sat in the back of the room and looked out of the window at schoolmates having fun in sports," Loretta recalls. "They said I was mentally retarded and couldn't compete. Then Special Olympics came and I began to run. My coach taught me how to go further and faster and now I can run the marathon in just over three hours. I have confidence in myself and know I can do almost anything I set out to do."

California Special Olympics added a third state competition—the Sports Classic, held in Berkeley—joining the Summer Games, held in Los Angeles and the Winter Games, held in Lake Tahoe. The Sports Classic was initiated to round out Special Olympics' seasonal sports plan, offering a cycle of training, local and area competitions, then finally statewide competitions in major sports for each season. The six fall sports covered in the Sports Classic included long-distance racing, powerlifting, roller skating, soccer, team bowling and volleyball. As with the Summer and Winter Games, volunteers played a major role in planning and implementing the Sports Classic.

1989

The Loma Prieta earthquake struck while America watched the Oakland A's and the San Francisco Giants play a World Series game at Candlestick Park. That tragic event overshadowed much in the country, including an important development for Special Olympics—"unified sports." Unified Sports was a program started by Special Olympics in Massachusetts, placing athletes with and without mental handicaps together on the same team. What was once denied to special athletes—the ability to compete with their peers, especially in a junior high or high school setting—was beginning to become a reality.

Unified Sports proved to be an invaluable tool for integrating people with mental retardation into the community at large. With special athletes included in "regular" national and world sports events, the door was opening for a quantum leap in achievements by Special Olympians. As special athletes received the same level and type of training that top level amateur athletes received, they knew the rules and were beginning to be able to compete comfortably outside the program.

Eighteen countries, represented by 1,055 athletes, competed in the International Special Olympics Games held at Reno-Lake Tahoe, Nevada.

Since its creation in 1980, the Directorate of International Development helped serve more

than 90 national Special Olympics programs in Europe, Africa, Latin America and the Far East by the end of the decade. In 1989, the Soviet Union, Hungary, Czechoslovakia and Indonesia requested assistance in setting up Special Olympics programs as well.

The Benefits of International Competition

There are many obvious rewards for special athletes participating in an international event. Participation can help athletes learn how to set goals and how to cope with success as well as failure. Training helps to build concentration and the ability to focus attention.

Some rewards are subtler. One of the subtle yet important rewards is the experience of traveling. When special athletes travel for competitive meets, their social skills are challenged in different ways. Traveling without parents helps to build independence and adds to self-confidence once they return home. Traveling and competing in different countries, athletes learn how to socialize with people from different backgrounds and cultures. Once home, they may feel more at ease in situations which earlier caused stress. The bottom line is that the experiences encountered while away from home empower the handicapped person and build confidence, which in turn impacts other parts of their lives.

One of the gymnastics events is vaulting. Loud applause greets an athlete as he makes his finishing pose.

OPPOSITE: A winner at any age. That's one of the great aspects of the program—it's life-long. You can always train and vie for the gold.

Paul Hoffman
Special Athlete, Basketball

Paul Hoffman, who is 35 years old, joined Special Olympics in 1983. Paul is a polished and enthusiastic public speaker. Here is the story of his involvement with Special Olympics in his own words:

"My mom found out about Orange County Special Olympics through a party or something that she attended where she got Madeline Evans' name (see Madeline's profile on page 58). I just called her one time and she gave me the name of Keith Brigman, who's now my coach. I talked with him and he said just come down to a practice. I came down and he just took a hold of me and got me a physical and I've been with the team ever since.

"Before, my life was very hard—just growing up and being accepted—because people thought that handicapped people, if they got around them, that it was like a disease and they would catch it and so I was really isolated. And I didn't really have many friends because no one really wanted to be associated with a handicapped person. So it was just very hard socializing because I always withdrew because I didn't feel like I fit in.

"Then with Special Olympics I started to feel more confident about myself and about being around people who had disabilities. Right now, I own my own place. I just bought a condo two years ago. I have a full-time job, so I put in 40 hours a week. I

drive my own vehicle and I'm basically just like a normal person. I gotta pay rent; I don't get any financial assistance or aid. I'm just making it out on my own. I have parents who are very supportive, so if I ever do need help I can lean back on them.

"But the main thing is that I'm making it in this real world. Maybe in a sense, I'm a role model, if I can say that, to some at Special Olympics. I'm an equipment manager at a local high school and I take care of all the equipment and issuing and getting sporting events ready—that's my job. I do speaking engagements for the state or for Orange County Special Olympics. Through the experience of doing some speaking, I've gotten to meet people in different companies and become friends with them; with my speaking ability and trying to express my feelings and sharing my experiences with Special Olympics, I'm trying to get people more involved.

"The most important message I have for people is that there's a place in this world for handicapped people outside of Special Olympics, in the working world. We can make a contribution to this world.

"I'm getting ready for basketball season right now. Hopefully, I will be at UCLA and vying for a gold medal. I've been team captain of my local chapter since I started, since I kinda know what's going on and am

like a coach on the floor. At Notre Dame, I was named team captain of the '87 International basketball team and in '91, I was named team captain of the handball team.

"I was a competitor; I am a competitor. I led the team in scoring and we ended up winning the bronze medal. We weren't picked to win a medal at all. I've gotten to go to Japan through Special Olympics. In 1987, right after I got back from Notre Dame, they wanted to send some athletes to Japan to promote Special Olympics and that was an experience. I threw the softball in track over there and it was just a different experience since I was one of the tallest ones walking around—I'm six-foot-five-and-a-half, and everyone was smaller than me. I was just impressed that everyone was very physically conscious about exercise, walking and riding bicycles to work. My biggest goal right now is that I'd like represent California at the 1995 International Games in Connecticut; that's my goal.

"For the rest of my life, somehow, someway, I'll be involved with Special Olympics. Even if I'm 80 years old, I'll be doing something, maybe walking the track or bowling. But as long as I can compete with the younger guys, I'll do that."

NEXT PAGE: Chris Donn shows perfect form as he hits the softball during the 1987 Summer Games.

Into the 1990s

NIA SPECIAL OLYMPIC
SPO
ON SHO
UMANITIES
CALIFORNIA
SPECIAL OLYMPICS
19
Kim
Bivens
ECHO

1990

The world order was in flux—Mrs. Shriver expressed it best when she wrote, "Special Olympics has been part of the wave of freedom and democracy that has swept Eastern Europe. Hungary and Czechoslovakia have joined Poland and Yugoslavia in the Special Olympics movement and will send athletes to the 1990 European Special Olympics Games this coming July. Most recently, the Soviet Union, including the republics of Latvia, Lithuania and Estonia, has become part of the worldwide Special Olympics family. Not only have the Soviets enthusiastically joined Special Olympics, but last February they hosted the largest coaches' clinic we have ever held." Because of the inclusion of the republics of the former USSR, Special Olympics International changed the name of its games to the Special Olympics World Summer and Winter Games.

Rafer Johnson continued to attend dozens of local Special Olympics meets each year around the country. His schedule increased over the years to the point where he conducted a minimum of 50 interviews annually, as well as presenting nearly 20 talks to civic clubs and other groups. In fact, the entire 20-plus members of the Johnson family were and continue to be involved in Rafer's Boutique, a tented shop at all the California Special Olympics Summer Games. All profits from the sale of items at Rafer's Boutique benefit the program.

The European Games were held during the summer in Strathclyde, Scotland. European special athletes numbering more than 2,500 came and competed.

OPPOSITE: Kim Bivens in the first-place spot on the awards platform during the 1985 Winter Games held at Echo Summit. This is the moment every athlete dreams of experiencing.

The '90s started with a bang as the Mount Kilimanjaro Confidence Climb was organized. Athletes from California Special Olympics were selected from a group of nominations to train and then to climb Mount Kilimanjaro. Training included the small-scale climbing of California's Mount Whitney.

1991

The 1991 Special Olympics World Summer Games were held in Minneapolis, Minnesota. A record 5,700 special athletes from 104 countries participated in the games. New sports and expanded events for existing sports were added. In aquatics, two lower level events, the 15-meter flotation and 15-meter walk, were added. Bocce was added as a new sport and competition took places in singles, doubles and mixed doubles events. In cycling, for the first time, a full range of events were offered, including a 40K marathon race. Also for the first time, a variety of western and English-style events were held, including *prix*

Special Athletes Compete Everywhere

- **Andy Leonard**, Special Olympics powerlifting athlete, was nominated for the Sullivan Award.

- **Lisa Elsener**, Kansas Special Olympics, was honored as an outstanding aquatics athlete by a swim club which includes U.S. National Team swimmers.

- **The U.S. Speed Skating Championships** have 16 special athletes competing.

- **The U.S. Figure Skating Championships** count eight special athletes as competitors.

- **The World Aquatics Championships** in Australia have six special athletes participating.

Two gymnasts share a special moment as they watch another athlete perform. The spirit of friendship is one of the most important aspects of participation in Special Olympics.

caprilli, which features jumping events. Ball hockey, the roller skating sport selected for the 1992 Olympics in Barcelona, was a demonstration sport. And there was a noted increase in participation in women's basketball. At the World Games, special athletes competed alongside regular athletes in Unified Sports, with competition held in basketball, bowling,

OPPOSITE: Safe at third! This athlete's thumbs-up sign has everyone in the stands cheering him home.

soccer, softball, team handball and volleyball.

The Sports Partnership Program was introduced by Special Olympics and the Los Angeles Unified School District in 1991, creating a new AA team within high school varsity and junior varsity regular teams. Four high schools participated in the program during the first year, providing side-by-side sports training, practice and competition for athletes with and without mental retardation. The AA team members traveled, wore the same uniforms

Arnold Schwarzenegger helps Dominique Davalos and Julie Flahavan celebrate a powerlifting victory at the International Games.

and were eligible to earn school letters. The athletes also participated in sport banquets and yearbook pictures. Interaction between special education and regular education athletes was geared toward making the schools' student bodies more aware of the students with special needs and their real accomplishments and true abilities. The program is

OPPOSITE: A bowler waits anxiously, hoping for a strike, during the Summer Games.

currently in effect in 28 schools in California. Other states are looking at instituting similar programs.

1992

Rafer Johnson stepped down after ten years of serving as President of the California Special Olympics Board of Directors, prompting Eunice Kennedy Shriver to create a new title for him as Special Olympics Ambassador. Rafer also continued to be a very active participant as the California

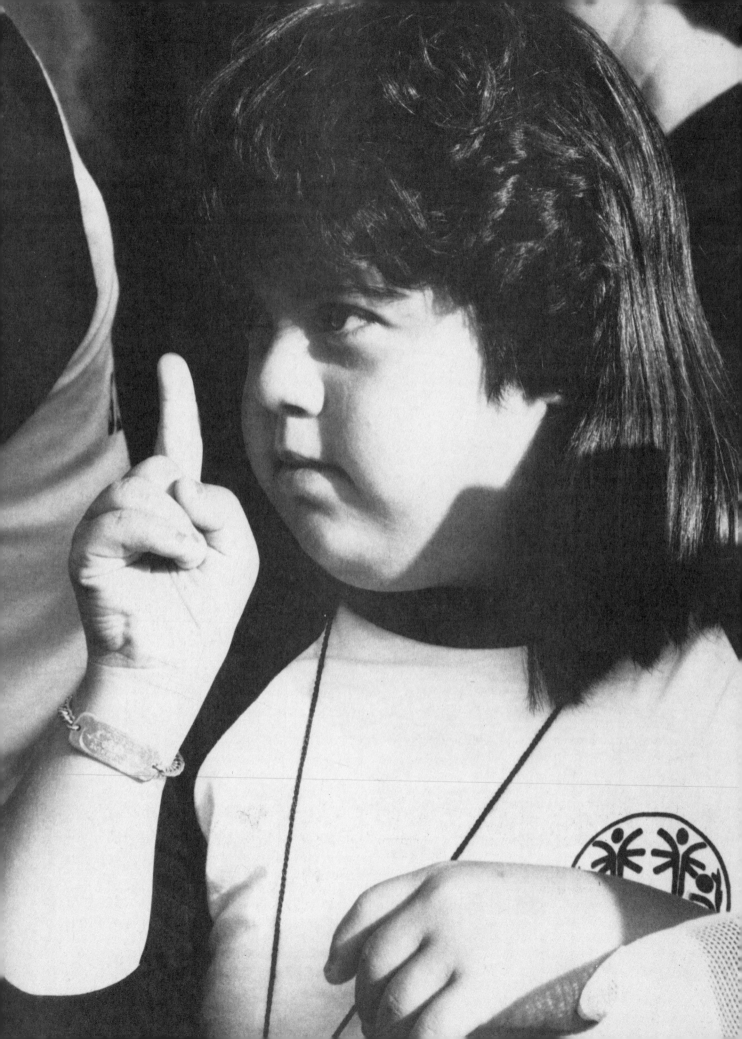

Fun at the Summer Games, as a relay team cheers at the end of their race.

Special Olympics' Chairman of the Board of Governors.

In California alone, more than 300 statewide competitions were held, not including the more than 1,500 local competitions. For the most visible of the statewide competitions, Prime Ticket produced a one-hour special program,

OPPOSITE: Everybody at Special Olympics is number one. As you walk around at an event, athletes and volunteers give each other the "We're number one" spirit, making it feel like one big family.

hosted by Steve Garvey and Christina Ferrara, highlighting the 1992 California Special Olympics Summer Games.

Millions of people watched the 1992 Winter Olympic Games televised from Albertville, France.

Andy Leonard of State College, Pennsylvania won a gold medal in the dead-lift competition in the 114-pound class at the American Drug Free Powerlifting Association national championships, making him the first special athlete to be a national titlist in open competition.

The world watched as Los Angeles burned in riots fueled by the outrage over the Rodney King verdict. One week later at Jackie Robinson Stadium, just blocks from the riots' flash point, nearly 500 athletes and 300 volunteers participated in the Los Angeles City Special Olympics Games.

Special Olympics athletes also competed in an exhibition event at the U.S. Track and Field Olympic Trials in New Orleans.

1993

The 1993 Special Olympics World Winter Games took place in Schladming-Salzburg, Austria, held for the first time ever outside the United States. Sixty countries sent 1,550 athletes to compete in 22 sports; all but two European countries sent athletes to participate in the games. Sweden, the Netherlands and South Africa, newcomers to Special Olympics, also attended.

The excitement of the athletes and volunteers who were traveling to Europe, some for the first time, had been growing since the games' location was announced. Athletes returned home with addresses of new friends and pen pals, photographs of their visit to Austria and memories of the fun they had while competing. Everyone, athletes and volunteers alike, also returned home with a deep sense of fulfillment and heightened self-confidence.

Events at the Austrian Winter Games included alpine skiing, cross-country skiing, figure skating, floor hockey and speed skating. Since skiing and speed skating were introduced at the first International Winter Games in 1977, athletes had grown increasingly proficient at these events. To continue to challenge them, a 10K cross-country event and a 1,000-meter speed skating event were added.

The impact of Special Olympics was proving just as strong in some countries in the '90s as it was in the United States in the '60s and '70s. A study of the '93 Special Olympics World Winter Games included a section on reactions of the people of Schladming-Salzburg, Austria. These cities offered schooling, treatment and residential services for the handicapped, but only in segregated settings. Schoolchildren and adults who were interviewed indicated they did not know where Austrians with disabilities went to school, where they worked or even where they lived. After the games, some of the schoolchildren interviewed said they were surprised to see that there was really not much difference between them and the special athletes.

In Austria, Special Olympics had much the same impact as it had and continues to have in the United States and around the world—it opened hearts and minds. When people see what people with mental retardation can do, how capable they are in many settings and how much courage and joy they bring to the situations which challenge them, they can't help but feel a sense of kinship with them.

In the United States, 1993 saw Special Olympics continuing its efforts to reach a wider segment of the general population and to help educate people to the realities of mental retardation. A Special Olympics 25th Anniversary Tour van, containing a multimedia traveling exhibit, was assembled to celebrate the progress of the program. The van was scheduled for stops in 70 cities, taking 14 months to

OPPOSITE: Cycling is a relatively new sport to the Specials Olympics program, but it has grown popular quickly. This special athlete is seen participating in the 1991 Cycling Championships.

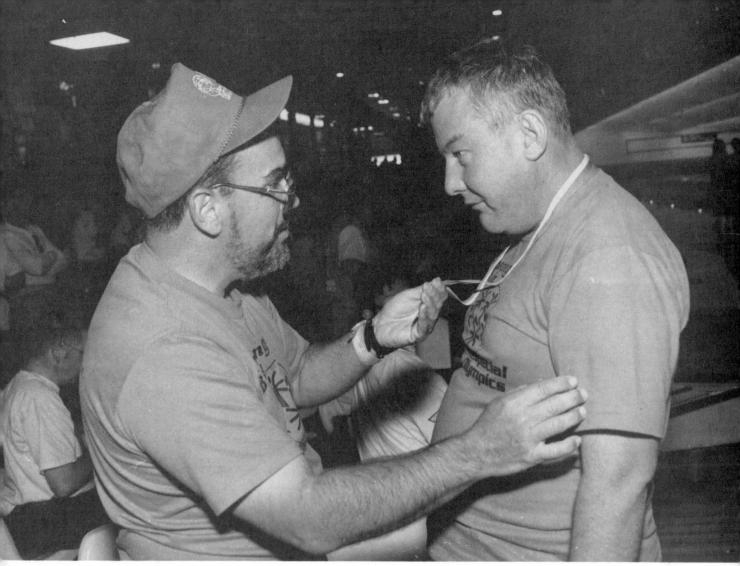

A coach and athlete share some time together after the awards presentation for medals in bowling.

cover the country. The tour was set to end in 1995 in New Haven, at the 1995 Special Olympics World Summer Games.

A walk through the exhibit gives a glimpse into the world of Special Olympics: It's hard to walk away from it without feeling the warmth and the struggle, the sharing and the love that are at the core of the program. Someone seeing this exhibit who has never spoken with a handicapped person or has never been involved with the program can't help but realize Special Olympics is not about "those poor kids." It's about people who are challenged. Some of their challenges may be more obvious than the challenges many of us face—but the difficulty of meeting any challenge is a universal experience. The exhibit highlights the universality of the courage of special athletes in facing of these challenges.

OPPOSITE: Concentration and poise before action—a gymnast mentally prepares himself before his performance.

Andy Leonard
Special Athlete, Powerlifting

"Small of body, big of heart" is what Andy Leonard's Special Olympics coach says of him. At five feet and 114 pounds, most people would guess that his sport is swimming or gymnastics. Even people who know sports wouldn't guess easily that Andy is a championship weightlifter who can dead lift four times his body weight. Andy is rated number two in the United States for powerlifters in the 114-pound class—number two in the country, not just Special Olympics.

Andy's success and accomplishments are impressive by any standards, but they are even more remarkable when you know the story of his life. Andy was born in Vietnam in 1969 when the war was raging and the countryside was being battered by artillery attacks and napalm. As a baby, he contracted a high fever which left him mentally retarded. When Andy was three years old, his parents were killed during an artillery attack, orphaning him, his three sisters and his brother. Andy's sister took him to the An Lac orphanage. After that day, he never saw any members of his family again.

Andy was just one of thousands of children airlifted to America in 1976 immediately before the fall of Saigon. He was just seven years old, couldn't speak English and, because of his handicap, didn't speak Vietnamese very well. The placement process was difficult,

but Andy found a loving home with Richard and Irene Leonard in Lock Haven, Pennsylvania, becoming the fourth of the family's children.

Growing up, Andy's general health was poor. He was so weak that riding a tricycle was difficult and, in later years, he needed surgery for eardrum infections. But Andy worked hard and always made the most of every opportunity. At his local YMCA, he joined the swim team and qualified for the state meet in the breast stroke.

When he was in the 11th grade, Andy's family moved to State College, Pennsylvania. Adjusting to a new environment can be rough for any teenager, and Andy found it difficult to keep up in sports with the other students in his new school. He spent most of the year just watching from the sidelines.

During this period, Andy's special education teacher introduced him to Special Olympics. Andy trained hard and seemed to blossom under the guidance of coaches, teachers and friends of Special Olympics. One coach, Clyde Doll, met Andy at some events and took note of his eagerness to compete. After talking with Andy, Coach Doll suggested he try powerlifting. The rest, as they say, is history. Andy jumped into the sport, working hard on technique and following an intense training program to increase his strength.

Andy's training and hard work paid off, producing bronze, silver and gold medals in event after event. At the 1991 International Summer Special Olympics Games in Minneapolis, Andy triumphed with a gold medal. His triumphs have extended beyond the world of Special Olympics, as Andy has distinguished himself as a champion powerlifter in open competition on the national scene as well. In 1992, Andy scored a gold medal in the American Drug Free Powerlifting Association national championships, making him the top powerlifter in his weight class in the United States.

Mark Arrowood
Special Athlete

In 1992, Americans cheered on speed skater Dan Jansen as he attempted to capture a gold medal. Interviewers at Albertville repeatedly asked Dan how he felt after Calgary; Dan still found it hard to focus on competition. Four years earlier, the country cried with Dan Jansen as he fell and lost the gold at the 1988 Winter Olympics Games in Calgary. The day before that race, he had learned that his sister, Jane, had died, losing her long battle with leukemia. Again, at Albertville, Dan came away empty handed.

Mark Arrowood, a Special Olympics athlete from Pennsylvania, was cheering Dan Jansen, too. After the Albertville games, Mark had written to Dan, athlete to athlete, about his own personal experience. Mark had competed in a Special Olympics event only weeks after his father had passed away.

He knew how hard it was to focus through the grief and loss. Even though Mark had won his competition, he knew how empty it was measured against the loss of a loved one. That's why Mark wrote to Dan and reminded him of the Special Olympics motto, "Let me win. But if I cannot win, let me be brave in the attempt." Mark also sent Dan one of his own Special Olympics gold medals for "being brave in the attempt."

Moved by what Mark had written to him, Dan Jansen arranged to meet Mark to thank him. "This has had more impact on me than anything else," Dan said of Mark's letter and gold medal. "It has helped me channel my grief. Mark will be my friend forever."

David Robinson
Special Athlete, Swimming

The stories of Special Olympics do not always culminate with accomplishments in competition. In fact, the skills learned in Special Olympics often translate into success in other areas of participants' lives, and victories can be won off the playing field as well as on. David Robinson of Sonora, California is definitely a case in point.

Dave worked hard in Special Olympics to develop his swimming skills. He counts two gold and three bronze medals in statewide competitions as some of his greatest awards.

But Dave's greatest swimming achievement had nothing to do with competition. There was something more precious than a gold medal at stake. The saving of a life depended on Dave's skill as a swimmer.

Dave, who has Down syndrome, was visiting the home of his best friend, Ronnie. Ronnie has a pool in his backyard which Dave uses. Ronnie's wife, Kimberly, was cleaning the deck near the pool while their two-year-old son Casey played nearby.

As Kimberly turned her back for a brief second, Casey fell from the edge of the pool and into the water without warning.

Dave watched in horror as the tiny boy hit the water and started to sink beneath the surface. Within seconds, Dave leapt to his feet, jumped into the pool and reached little Casey. He pulled the child to him, then managed to swim back to the surface. Casey was coughing and scared, but otherwise unharmed thanks to Dave Robinson's quick and decisive action.

To this day, Ronnie believes it was more than just luck and coincidence that his best friend was just a few steps away when Casey's life was in danger.

Larry Robbins
Special Athlete, Basketball

At 19 years old, and after only four years participating in Special Olympics, Larry Robbins has at least 30 medals in his room. He also has found something else to be treasured in Special Olympics: a community.

His mother Rhoda remembers discovering Special Olympics: "I was looking for an after-school program. Someone told me about a basketball program and I thought it was a Parks and Recreation program, but it turned out to be Special Olympics. I took Larry down to the courts and he started playing basketball.

"I'm surprised when I watch him," Rhoda continues. "I don't even know the rules of basketball, yet he does. The program has given him confidence in himself and he's learned socialization skills. Most of his friends participate in one form or another of Special Olympics. Tuesday night he plays basketball, Thursday night he goes to powerlift and Saturday morning he goes bowling. It's given him a sense of belonging somewhere. It gives him a sense of belonging to a team and that's important for everyone.

"Before Special Olympics, when Larry was younger, I watched him play with neighborhood kids and they would outgrow him. He was getting older and playing with kids who were younger and younger. I'd want him to play with age-appropriate kids, but 17-year-old kids didn't want to play with him. I remember when the neighborhood kids would go to softball practice and Larry would go as well. I would go to pick Larry up and he'd always be sitting there—on the bench, watching. And he sat there and he watched. And I never figured he'd get the chance to be the kid out there on the field.

"Now, even for me, I get that thrill of watching him put on the uniform and go out there and play," Rhoda says. "It's terrific. I waited a very long time for that. He's so proud when he comes home from a tournament. It's given him a true idea of what it's like to grow up."

While Larry now lives at home with his mother Rhoda and stepfather Dan Hornback, his goal is to live independently. Part of working toward that goal includes attending a school where he learns job skills. Larry has worked at Marshall's as part of his school's retail sales training program. He has also taken and especially enjoyed classes in food service, including a stint working in the Holiday Inn banquet room.

"I love Special Olympics," Larry says. "I'm doing some softball, soccer, powerlifting, but I like basketball best. I do push-ups, sit-ups and I work out. I like running and jumping. My coaches help me a lot."

Paul C. Boyle
Special Athlete, Equestrian

Paul Boyle is 26 years old and lives at home with his parents, Barbara and Kevin. He has an older brother and a sister-in-law, David and Lisa. Paul has been in the Special Olympics program for six years now and competes in athletics, soccer and equestrian events. In fact, horseback riding is a favorite sport of Paul's, a result of his ten-year involvement with a program called Ahead With Horses, an Orange County nonprofit organization that gives people with mental and physical handicaps the opportunity to work with horses.

Paul also has a job a lot of people would love—working as a freelance production assistant in the film industry. (His mother is also involved in the industry as a producer.) This has given Paul the opportunity to travel and build up his flag collection. Some of the films Paul has worked on include *My Left Foot*, *Love Crimes* and *The Field*. Always on the go, he also has been studying karate for the past three years.

Kevin, Paul's father and speech coach, remembers that Paul first heard about Special Olympics while he was attending St. Vincent/Seton School in Santa Barbara for the developmentally disabled.

"It's been great for Paul," Kevin says. "His brother was always in Little League and soccer and Paul wasn't. He felt left out. Now he gets to compete with his own peers, his own friends. And his family and

friends come out and cheer him on. Since Special Olympics, Paul has grown in self esteem and he feels good about himself—just getting out, competing, making friends makes all the difference.

"When Paul was younger, his life was focused on gaining control of his epilepsy. It took a very long time to get the right medication and now he's about 99 percent in control. The biggest story about Paul is his work with Ahead With Horses. He started with them to improve his posture and today he stands

completely straight."

According to Paul, what he really loves about Special Olympics is "helping other athletes. I encourage them to think positive thoughts. I try to help them with learning the Special Olympics oath—I believe in the oath. Special Olympics is like a big family. We help one another to accomplish things. I have a lot of fun. My goal is to get more athletes and volunteers involved in Special Olympics. And also to get my ninth gold medal at state games!"

The Athletic Events

In 1968, track-and-field and swimming were the first two official sports offered by Special Olympics. Today, Special Olympics athletes train and compete year-round in 23 Olympic-style events which have been adapted to the needs of the special athlete. As in the Olympics, events are introduced in training and then added to the competitive schedule. The list of sports continues to grow. Golf, the newest sport to be added to the program, premieres at the 1995 Special Olympics World Summer Games in New Haven, Connecticut.

Athletics

Athletics, or track-and-field, is the heart of the Special Olympics program, as it is in the Olympics. Running, jumping and throwing are the basic human motions and, consequently, the core of all other sports. Athletic events tested speed, endurance, agility and power even before the ancient Olympic Games in Greece. In those games, the *stade* was the only athletics event and the most popular contest. Participants raced the length of the stadium, nearly 200 meters (600 feet), to determine the fastest athlete. Early forms of jumping and throwing were also later developed at Olympia, Greece. The following briefly describes the events which comprise the Special Olympics athletic competitions.

Track

The 50-meter and 100-meter sprints test sheer speed. Grace, power, relaxation and control are the keys to achieving the fastest

OPPOSITE: The winner of a track-and-field event at the 1991 International Special Olympics Summer Games in Minneapolis after crossing the finish line.

speed. This course is a straight-line race from start to finish. The 200-meter sprint is a challenge in both technique and endurance. This sustained sprint of half a lap involves running around a turn and making the adjustments to negotiate the change from a straight sprint. The 400-meter sprint is said to be a race run on sheer willpower. To sprint at close to maximum speed on a straightaway and around turns for 400 meters requires power and physical and mental conditioning. Hurdling is fast sprinting over barriers. This event was added to the Special Olympics in 1992. The hurdles are exciting for both participant and observer as runners clear three-foot barriers while maintaining a consistent running stride.

The distance events include the 800-, 1,500- and 5,000-meter runs. The distance runner is the ultimate athlete. Runners who compete in these events have well-trained cardiovascular systems. In addition to strong hearts and lungs, mental willpower and confidence are needed to finish the race. The toughest distance race is the 26-mile marathon, named to honor the famous Greek messenger, Pheidippides, who ran from the plains of Marathon to Athens to announce victory.

Walking events were introduced to provide a lifetime competitive sport for athletes of all ages and abilities. Race walking, fast becoming a popular fitness activity, is defined as a succession of steps in which the advancing foot must touch the track before the rear foot leaves. Race walking events cover distances from 25 meters to 15,000 meters.

Teamwork is vital in both the 4x100-meter relay and the 4x400-meter relay since the race is won by the four fastest individuals who work together to coordinate a series of smooth

It's a close race for these three wheelchair athletes during the 1983 Summer Games.

exchanges of a ten-and-a-half-inch baton.

For athletes whose mobility is enhanced by the use of a wheelchair, there are a series of events for manually-powered and mechanically-powered wheelchairs. Competition is held in sprinting, distance and obstacle races. These competitions require training and strategies similar to non-wheelchair events.

Field

The high jump became popular with the development of the foam landing area. The "flop," a jump technique which came to be used in the late 1960s, was easily adapted by Special Olympics athletes with great success.

The long jump requires sprint speed and jumping ability. The participant runs at full speed up to a designated mark, then jumps through the air as far as possible. In the standing long jump, the participant starts in a full standing position, then take two steps before jumping.

The shot put is a test of total body control. A shot (an eight-pound, 13-ounce ball) is put (or thrown) from the confines of a seven-foot ring. The goal is to put the shot over the greatest distance. This event requires a variety of techniques to harness both power and control.

The softball throw of Special Olympics is most akin to the Olympic javelin throw. In this event, the thrower runs to the line, ending

Summer Games swimmers prepare to hit the water at the judge's signal.

with a solid plant in the ground as the ball is thrown.

The pentathlon has its roots in the ancient Olympics pentathlon and the modern Olympic decathlon. The Special Olympics pentathlon events are the 100-meter sprint, 400-meter run, long jump, shot put and high jump. The performances in each event are measured against a scoring table and added, with the highest cumulative score winning.

Aquatics

Aquatics is the international term for the Special Olympics sports of swimming and diving. Competitive swimming is a rela-tively new sport and dates to the 19th century and the advent of swimming pools. In the early days of modern Olympics, only four swimming events were sanctioned—breaststroke, back-stroke, crawl or freestyle and butterfly.

Special Olympics held its first swimming event at the Chicago Special Olympics in 1968 and has grown to include 15 events with distances from 100 meters to 1,500 meters. Competitive diving first appeared on the program of the 1972 Los Angeles Third Inter-national Summer Special Olympics Games. Athletes were required to perform both com-pulsory and optional dives from a one-meter springboard.

Terry Wright bowls a strike during the 1992 California Special Olympics Summer Games.

Basketball

Basketball is the rare sport which has exclusively American roots. It was invented in 1891 at the YMCA in Springfield, Massachusetts by Dr. James Naismith. The goal was to create a game which could be played indoors during the winter months. The "baskets" were two peach baskets with the bottoms cut off which were nailed at opposite ends of the gym. Astonishingly, 12 of Dr. Naismith's 13 basic rules are still in place today.

The first Special Olympics games in 1968 featured a basketball clinic taught by players

OPPOSITE: Before the game, a special athlete warms up with a few lay-up shots.

of the Chicago Bulls team. In Los Angeles at the 1972 games, basketball was first included as an official Special Olympics sport. In 1974, the National Basketball Association and the American Basketball Association joined to sponsor the National Special Olympics Basketball Program, which included team play and Run, Dribble and Shoot competitions.

Bowling

Mention is made of bowling as far back as 5200 B.C., but it was not until the 19th century that the sport enjoyed general popularity. During the 1950s, innovative automatic pin-setting equipment was developed, which transformed bowling into one of America's

Rebecca Nerney and her coach wait for her scores during the 1991 International Special Olympics Games equestrian competition.

favorite sports.

For Special Olympics athletes, bowling is a sport which can be played year-round, life-long. In the Special Olympics program, bowling is one of the top three sports in athlete participation.

Cycling

Count de Sivrac attached two wheels to a crossbar and propelled himself across the ground with his feet. That primitive 1790 design was the first bicycle. In 1839, a Scottish blacksmith added cranks and improved the

OPPOSITE: Bill from San Luis Obispo Special Olympics rides his warm-up lap before competing in the 1991 Cycling Championships.

steering mechanism. Then John Dunlop gave us the first air-filled tire. By 1870, bicycle racing was a sport.

Special Olympics introduced cycling competition with a road course event at the 1987 International Summer Special Olympics Games in Indiana.

Equestrian

The pairing of man and horse dates to the Bronze Age, more than 4,000 years ago. Equestrian competitions of horse-and-chariot racing were part of the ancient Olympic Games in 680 B.C. In the Middle Ages, dressage developed as an event which tests movement,

Volunteer judges, well wishers and teammates watch an exciting soccer match during the 1986 Summer Games.

execution and horse-rider communication. The English aristocracy and their love of fox-hunting can be credited as the sources of jumping events. With equestrian history so rich, it was natural that these competitions would be included in the program of the 1912 Olympic Games held in Stockholm, Sweden.

Special Olympics athletes compete in the events of dressage, equitation, pole bending and barrel racing, drill teams, *prix caprilli*, showmanship and team relays.

Figure Skating

Ice skating is believed to have started in Scandinavia sometime during the second century when bone and wood were tooled together to be used for travel on frozen streams and across ponds. It wasn't until after the 1850s, when ice skates evolved from iron blades to steel ones with leather straps and clamps for attachment to regular shoes, that ice skating caught on as a sport. Ice skating became so popular by 1896 that it was included in the program for the first modern Winter Olympic Games.

In 1977, Special Olympics added figure skating competition at the first International

A special athlete flashes a winning smile from the sidelines. Even off the field, she's having a ball.

Winter Special Olympics Games at Steamboat Springs, Colorado. In singles and pairs competition, skaters perform a short program incorporating required movements to music of their own choosing, then follow with a long program of personally choreographed moves. Ice dancing pairs compete in compulsory-dance and free-dance programs. Scoring is based on technical merit, presentation and style.

Football (Soccer)

Soccer is the world's most popular sport. An estimated 120 million people play the game. Some speculate that soccer or football can be traced as far back as 600 B.C. to the Japanese game of *kemari* or to the pre-Columbian ball games of Central and South America. Regardless, a direct line can be traced to the ball games of the British Isles in the first century. The game rules for soccer as we know it were established in 1848 and are overseen by the Football Association, which was created in 1863. Soccer was first played in the 1900 Olympic Games held in Paris, France.

Special Olympics added soccer to its program for the 1983 international competitions in Baton Rouge.

A gymnastics floor exercise performance highlights an athlete's skill and training. Here, perfect form is achieved and captured for all to see.

Gymnastics

There were gymnastics clubs in Europe in the 1850s; however, the first international competition did not take place until it was an official Olympic sport on the program for the first modern Olympic Games held in Athens, Greece in 1896. It was an exclusively male sport until 1928, when women's gymnastics was officially added. The current popularity of gymnastics is most likely due to worldwide television exposure.

Special Olympics gymnastics, tumbling and

OPPOSITE: The rings event is one of the most difficult competitions in gymnastics. This routine is going very well, judging by the look on the coach's face.

free exercise, were introduced in 1972 as competitive events at the Third International Special Olympics Games in Los Angeles. Today, athletes compete in all the Olympic gymnastic events. Women's events include: artistic gymnastics events of vault, uneven parallel bars, balance beam, floor exercise and rhythmic gymnastics. Men's events include: floor exercise, pommel horse, rings, vault, parallel bars, and high or horizontal bar.

Floor Hockey

Stick-and-ball games may very well have been the first type of sports. Even in Egyp-

A powerlifter from Alabama at the 1991 Special Olympics Summer World Games. Professional scoreboards, equipment, judging and competitors from all around the world add to the excitement.

tian tombs there are relief carvings of a game which resembles a form of hockey. There's some evidence that the Aztecs may have played a similar game. And during the Middle Ages, the French game of *hocquet* was popular.

Today, the games we know in Special Olympics are hybrids of the popular ice hockey. Floor hockey (played with hockey-type sticks and a puck) and poly hockey (played with special plastic-blade sticks and a ball) have been adapted for play in a gymnasium or on a concrete surface. Floor hockey was played at the first Chicago Special Olympics between teams from Canada and the United States, demonstrating that Special Olympics athletes

could learn and compete in team sports requiring individual skills and, most importantly, team-play skills.

Powerlifting

Although the early Greeks exercised with lead and stone dumbbells, weightlifting was not a competitive event in the ancient Olympics. Weightlifting as a competitive sport with game rules started in Germany and quickly spread throughout Europe. Weightlifting, the Olympic counterpart to Special Olympics' powerlifting, was one of the sports on the program for the inaugural modern

Dominique Davalos in the dead-lift competition at the 1989 Special Olympics Powerlifting Championship.

Olympic Games of 1896.

Special Olympics powerlifters compete in the bench press and the dead lift. Powerlifting scoring is based on the weight multiplied by a coefficient assigned by the lifter's body weight. This allows lifters of varying sizes to compete equally while lifting different weight amounts.

Roller Skating

An easy pastime, ever popular with children, roller skating is also a competitive sport worldwide. Although not an Olympic sport, speed skating and artistic skating have been around since the early 1900s.

In Special Olympics, artistic skating encompasses three events: school figures, freestyle singles and dance. In roller speed skating, events include races of 100 meters to 500 meters, as well as relays and slalom.

Sailing

Sailboat racing is as old as the boats themselves. Although sailing has been an Olympic sport since 1896, sailing will appear for the first time as an event in 1995 at the Special Olympics World Games in New Haven, Connecticut with competition in two- and four-person crew races.

A special athlete lets the pitch fly during a 1987 Summer Games softball game.

Skiing

Skiing is one of humankind's oldest forms of transportation. Primitive art in northern climates depicts skiing scenes. Skiing originated as a competitive sport in Norway in 1840. The introduction of the sport into the alpine regions of Switzerland, France and Italy ignited popular interest. Skiing generally takes two forms: alpine skiing (commonly called downhill) and nordic or cross-country skiing.

In the Special Olympics program, there are three alpine skiing events: the downhill, the slalom and the giant slalom. Nordic skiing events cover cross-country distances from 25 meters to 10,000 meters. As in track events, skiers with the lowest elapsed times in their division are the winners.

Softball

Think softball—picnics and parks come to mind. Invented originally as an indoor game, by George Hancock in 1887, softball clearly has its origins in baseball. It's been called indoor baseball, kitten ball, mush ball or playground ball, but in 1926, when it moved

OPPOSITE: Greg Helsten from California Special Olympics on the slopes in a downhill skiing event at Lake Tahoe.

Team handball action at an International Games competition. Focus and strength are key requirements for the game.

outdoors, it was renamed softball. The first national championships were held in Chicago at the 1933 World's Fair. The Amateur Softball Association continues to petition to have softball added as an official sport to the Olympic Summer Games program. Currently, it is a demonstration sport event.

Softball premiered in 1979 at the International Summer Special Olympics Games held in Brockport, New York.

OPPOSITE: A speed skater races for the finish line during the 1989 International Winter Games in Reno, Nevada. Modification of standard equipment includes knee pads, gloves and a head-face guard helmet.

Speed Skating

A cousin to figure skating, speed skating was developed at the same time as its slower, more elegant relative. It became a part of the Olympics program in the 1924 Winter Olympics in Chamonix, France.

Speed skating first entered the Special Olympics program at the first International Winter Olympics held at Steamboat Springs, Colorado.

Table Tennis

Table tennis is, without doubt, the most popular racquet sport in the world today. Like its outdoor cousin, tennis, the game

requires quick reflexes, nimble footwork and keen hand-eye coordination. Called ping-pong because of the sound the celluloid ball makes when bouncing off the table and paddle, Parker Brothers took out a U.S. patent in 1901 and helped popularize the game in North America. The first world championships were held in 1927; it was added as an official sport in the Olympic Games in 1988.

For Special Olympics athletes, table tennis is a demonstration sport which premiered at the 1987 International Special Olympics Games in Indiana.

Team Handball

Olympic team handball is a different sport from the two- or four-person handball found in the United States, and the word "team" was added to "handball" to help differentiate the two. Team handball is closer in concept and goal to water polo or soccer and requires many of the same skills needed for basketball. The roots of the game are found in Czechoslovakian *hazena*, German *torball* and Danish *handbold*, all of which were combined to facilitate international competition. In 1928, sport representatives from 11 nations drew up the rules for 11 players on each team. Scandinavian countries later developed a seven-a-side version. Seven-a-side team handball is the indoor sport which is played in Olympic competition today.

Special Olympics added team handball to its international competitions in 1991 at the International Summer Special Olympics Games in Minneapolis.

OPPOSITE: The ball scoots past a team handball goalie, scoring a point for the opposing team during the 1991 International Special Olympics Summer Games.

Tennis

Jeu de paume was a French handball game played by enthusiasts on an indoor court. When players decided to spare their hands by using ever more effective bats, rackets and balls, it evolved into the sport we recognize today. Tennis was included in the 1896 modern Olympic Games and remained until 1924, when it was removed due to a conflict between the International Olympic Committee and the International Tennis Federation. It was welcomed back as a demonstration sport in 1984 and achieved full medal status in 1988 at the Olympic Games in Seoul, Korea.

Special Olympics added tennis to their list of demonstration sports in 1987 at the International Special Olympics Games in Indiana.

Volleyball

Invented by YMCA director William G. Morgan in 1895, volleyball was first offered as an alternative to basketball, which was thought to be too strenuous for most people. Competitive volleyball has evolved from the leisurely, family-play game first developed into a smashing, diving, leaping ball game. Men's and women's volleyball were introduced as Olympic sports in 1964 during the Olympic Games held in Tokyo, Japan.

As a Special Olympics sport, team volleyball is played six-a-side and moves at a speedy pace, much like its Olympic version.

Brian F. Loeb
Special Athlete, Swimming

Many letters arrive daily at Special Olympics offices all around the world. One of the most moving letters received by California Special Olympics came from Lorraine Loeb, Brian's mother.

"The first time I held Brian in my arms, he looked like such a perfect baby. I was so relieved. You see, I had reason to worry. I had gotten polio early in my pregnancy, leaving me partially paralyzed. And during my difficult labor with Brian, my heart stopped three times. So when he arrived, looking so beautiful, I was the happiest mother in the world.

"But over the next months, it became plain that everything wasn't as perfect as I thought. Brian was slower at developing than his brother had been. Before long, the signs were all too clear. My son was mentally retarded.

"As Brian got older, things were kind of tough. He didn't speak; he'd just shake his head. In school, he was enrolled in special education classes. The 'normal' kids teased and bullied him.

"Then, when Brian was 14 years old, he got involved with Special Olympics. I remember his first event—a swimming race. It took him a full minute to cross the pool, but he finished. And he got a medal. He was a winner for the first time in his life. Sud-

denly, Brian felt just as good as his brothers. And he had the medal to prove it. From that moment on, he became a different person. He walked to school with his head high. He stopped hiding and began to talk. It was a real miracle.

"It made a change in me, too. I thought, if Brian could overcome his handicap, maybe I could do the same. So after many years in a wheelchair, I decided I would work to stand on my own. On the day he turned 18, Brian finished first in the 25-yard freestyle and won his first gold medal. The crowd was cheering and somebody started singing 'Happy Birthday' over the loudspeaker, and everyone

joined in. I stood up to sing along. It was the first time in 18 years that I stood alone. I can still see the look on Brian's face when he saw me. He started clapping his hands and yelling, 'You did it, Mom, You did it, Mom.'

"I'm a lucky mother to have a son like Brian. And I'm thankful that we both have Special Olympics. It's taught us that it isn't the strength of your body or mind that counts—it's the strength of your spirit."

Today, at 38, Brian has been involved with Special Olympics for 23 years and participates in swimming, floor hockey, downhill and cross-country skiing and bowling. Over the years, Brian has won 62 gold medals, six silver medals and two bronze medals—two of the gold and three of the silver have been medals won in international games competitions.

Brian feels that his biggest accomplishment outside of Special Olympics has been holding down a job and supporting himself for the last five years. He works at the Lakewood Center Mall as a maintenance person, but he's also a card-carrying Screen Actors Guild member. He has a movie, *Killing Stone*, and three Special Olympics commercials directed by Michael Landon to his credit.

Jeffrey White
Special Athlete, Half Marathon and Marathon

Jeffrey White is a 30-year-old special athlete who lives at home with his mother Charlene. He started with the Special Olympics swimming program when he was eight and through the years, he has accomplished a lot. He has danced the Nutcracker Ballet with the Daly City Dance Academy and maintains a karate blue belt status. But for the past 15 years, running has been Jeff's number one love and only hobby. And it is in running that Jeff has truly excelled.

It all started in late 1989, at a competitive meet. Charlene White and Pat Diskin, Jeff's athletics coach, started talking while Jeff was running in an event. The main topic was Jeff's vision impairment and how he had learned to functionally use his vision in different ways in order to see and get around. In fact, Jeff started karate classes initially to improve his balance.

Their talk about vision turned to dreams, and Charlene shared with Pat a dream Jeff had about running a marathon. She asked Pat if she thought it was within the realm of possibility. Pat Diskin has been Jeff's running coach for fifteen years, since the beginning of his training, and felt that Jeff had what it takes as an

Jeffrey White and his coach, Pat Diskin.

athlete to run a marathon.

With full family support behind him, Jeff left his garden crew position at a local sheltered workshop to train. Pat and Jeff worked together carefully to build a training schedule so that Jeff's dream could be realized. Over the next year, Jeff ran 10K races, worked with Pat on visually managing race courses and concurrently trained for and was chosen to compete in the 1991 International Special Olympics Games on his state team in athletics. At Minneapolis, Jeff ran the half marathon and was the first U.S. finisher, third overall—and a bronze

medalist.

In late 1991, an opportunity arose when an employee at the California Special Olympics office called Pat to say that she had someone who would sponsor an athlete in the Los Angeles Marathon, which was scheduled to be held in March, 1992. That someone would be Jeff. Pat and Jeff stepped up their already intensive training schedule.

In just three years, Jeff's dream to run a marathon came true when he completed the 1992 L.A. Marathon in just over three hours, finishing 330th in a field of 20,000. In the process, he qualified for the April 1993 Boston Marathon. In between the L.A. and Boston Marathons, Jeff ran the Portland Marathon in October 1992. He's still going strong and planning to run the 1994 Portland Marathon.

And what's in the future for Jeff White? His dream now is to have the full marathon placed for the first time on the 1995 Special Olympics World Summer Games event schedule so he can run his first Special Olympics marathon.

Jenny Skinner
Special Athlete, Equestrian

Twenty-three-year-old Jenny Skinner is a gifted athlete who has been involved with Special Olympics for 12 years. While in elementary school, she was lucky to be introduced to Special Olympics by Cathy Salzman and Bobbie Roberts, both of whom became her coaches. She started training and competing in soccer, floor hockey, softball, track-and-field and roller skating but now she concentrates on swimming, cross-country skiing and her biggest love—equestrian events.

Jenny has achieved much with Special Olympics. She was the 1989 Spirit of Friendship Award winner and an alternate for the equestrian team at the 1991 Special Olympics International Games, as well as an ongoing participant in the Special Olympics Outreach Program.

Her accomplishments outside of Special Olympics are equally impressive. In 1991, Jenny was invited to speak twice at University of California, Irvine for an audience of special education teachers. For the past several years, Jenny has had many opportunities to educate the public about the capabilities of handicapped riders through her involvement with the American Riding Club for the Handicapped.

Jenny lives at home with her parents, Paul and Marilyn Skinner. While she has no siblings, seven Japanese exchange students have lived with the family over the years.

Jenny says of her Special Olympics experience: "Special Olympics is special to me. It feels good inside of me. I have so much fun and make new friends and learn new sports. I can go to new places and do things like the rope course at camp...

"I am proud of my horse group. We go so many places and compete with other groups and I have learned so much about horses. I ride English and western. I am learning dressage and vaulting. We have a parade group, too. I ride three days a week and sometimes I can help with the little kids."

Larry Herschler, one of Jenny's Special Olympics coaches, says, "Jenny's dedication and enthusiasm are a true representation of the spirit of Special Olympics. Special Olympics has permitted Jenny to reach out into the community. Her participation has allowed her to exhibit her talents as an athlete and as a team player."

Jenny's mother, Marilyn, adds: "Special Olympics has given Jenny the opportunity to reach out into the community. Her poise and confidence have allowed her to develop and exhibit her talents as an athlete and a role model for younger athletes. As an Outreach representative, Jenny has expanded her ability to communicate and her natural friendship and sincerity shine through and draw in her audience. Jenny has developed friendships both within and outside of Special Olympics. Her goal is to continue informing the public of the capabilities of the mentally retarded and to see expansion of the Special Olympics program so more athletes can have the same opportunities Jenny has experienced."

Jonathan Buller
Special Athlete, Swimming

Jonathan Buller and his coach, Betty Lyman.

At 24, Jonathan has done more than anyone ever expected. Jonathan likes to give his parents, Vern and Marlys, and his sister Brenda, a reason to be proud of his accomplishments. As an active swimmer, he gives them plenty of opportunities.

Eight years ago, Jonathan was swimming at a public pool with a friend who was involved with Special Olympics. Jonathan's friend invited him to attend a Special Olympics swimming event. He went and has been involved with the program ever since.

Not only has he competed in Special Olympics events, bringing home gold medals from two Special Olympics International Games, but his talents were great enough to compete and win a gold medal in the U.S. Olympic Festival '90, an event hosted by the United States Olympic Committee.

When he's not in the pool or working, Jonathan loves to draw or play Nintendo. Betty Lyman, Jonathan's coach, says, "Jonathan has developed socially, emotionally and physically since he has become part of Special Olympics. He is an inspiration to us all. He is one great athlete and a joy to be with."

Julie Flahavan
Special Athlete, Powerlifting

Powerlifter Julie Flahavan is a 23-year-old who was introduced to Special Olympics when she was in high school. In just five years, Julie has quickly moved through the powerlifting program to become a top performer. Julie was named Most Inspirational Athlete of the 1987 California Special Olympics Summer Games.

Her coach Judy says Julie's early interest and dedication make her a pioneer in women's powerlifting.

"Imagine a little 112-pound girl bench pressing 115 pounds and dead lifting 205 pounds—that's Julie."

That's why she was a gold medal winner at the 1991 International Special Olympics Summer Games in Minneapolis. Julie herself says, "It's a lot of fun. I'm learning a lot about powerlifting. Judy is a good coach."

Julie is the youngest daughter of Rose and Tom Flahavan. She has three brothers, Dan, John and Tom, and one sister, Carolyn. You won't just find Julie in the gym—she is also active in square dancing.

Richard Dunning
Special Athelete, Powerlifting

"I want to enjoy life. I like to get out and meet people and, of course, keep my health," says 47-year-old powerlifter Richard Dunning. "I love the challenge of Special Olympics. I get my body in good physical form. I refuse to be a couch potato. I have had the greatest time."

Dolores Dunning, Richard's mother, feels just as strongly as her son about the program. "Special Olympics is by far the most wonderful thing that has ever happened to Richard," she says. "It is a valuable experience

for him. He is who he is because of Special Olympics." Richard's brother, Robert, and his sister, Dolores Guffey, are also very proud of their brother's accomplishments.

Richard has been involved with Special Olympics for 20 years. It's been 20 years full of accomplishment, including a silver medal for baseball won at the International Games in Notre Dame in 1987.

Pat Diskin, one of Richard's coaches, says, "Richard is one of the finest athletes I have ever

had the privilege of working with. He is self-motivated, takes instruction and criticism with the right attitude and shows honest concern for the well-being of himself and other athletes. Richard's self esteem and confidence have grown tremendously because of his participation in the program."

In 1989, Richard was honored with Special Olympics' Spirit of Friendship award.

Looking to the Future—
1995 and Beyond

Today Special Olympics serves one-third of the mentally retarded persons who could gain valuable skills from sport training and competition. Thousands of special athletes have gone beyond Special Olympics and are in the vocational, social and recreational mainstream of society. And Special Olympics is growing, as more athletes participate and as the program refines and expands the sports offered.

Special Olympics is now the largest amateur sports organization in the world. There are programs operating in 120 countries and in all 50 American states. Internationally, there are approximately half a million children and adults with mental retardation who participate in Special Olympics.

During the '90s, more than 350 competitions will be held annually throughout the state of California. In between competitive meets, there will be Community Sports Training Camps where athletes meet with coaches and clinicians to sharpen individual form and generate team camaraderie. Skills developed at these camps find their way into competition and into the community.

Today, Special Olympics provides technical, strategic and philosophical training to coaches in all 23 winter and summer Olympic sports. It also provides extensive training materials, including the Sports Skills Instructional Program, a methodical and creative training regimen for the athletes featuring "skill progression lessons." Each sport has a Sports Skills Guide which demonstrates the teaching and learning progressions for each sport by breaking each single skill into sub-tasks. This allows special athletes to become proficient in

OPPOSITE: Arnold Schwarzenegger with powerlifting twins Mark and Mike Hembd.

Number of Special Olympics Athletes Worldwide

- Africa—20,165 athletes
- Asia/Pacific Rim—79,075 athletes
- Canada—16,000 athletes
- Caribbean—5,272 athletes
- Europe—249,949 athletes
- Latin America—125,200 athletes
- Middle East—3,670 athletes
- United States—438,549 athletes

a skill based on the mastery of sub-tasks.

In 1993, over 25,000 coaches were trained and certified in the United States as Special Olympics coaches. Since its initiation in 1981, over 200,000 coaches have completed the 18-hour Special Olympics Coaches' Training and Certification Program.

The 1995 Special Olympics World Summer Games will be held from July 1-9, in New Haven, Connecticut. These games are expected to be the largest sports event in the world in 1995—with 6,500 special athletes, 2,000 coaches, 15,000 family members and 45,000 volunteers participating. Athletes are training and competing in area, regional and state meets in the hopes of qualifying for their state team.

In 25 years, Special Olympics has helped to inspire significant and profound changes in the way society perceives and acts toward people with mental retardation. However, the work of Special Olympics is far from over and the figures reveal that the journey isn't even close to a quarter complete. There are 190 million people with mental retardation or three-and-a-

The love and support of a celebrity like J.C. Parrish, former Platters member, makes all the difference to the athletes. Celebrities attend competitions to award medals, sign autographs and give hugs.

half percent of the world population, only 940,000 of whom participate in Special Olympics. Today, just in California, there are over 100,000 children and adults with mental retardation and only approximately 25,000 are Special Olympics athletes. That means that just in California more than 75,000 people with developmental disabilities are still not experiencing the possibility of being the best that they can be.

And the numbers are not going to decrease. Even with the money and research going toward identification of the causes of mental

OPPOSITE: Dick Sargent, a dedicated volunteer since the beginning of the program, takes a moment to chat with a special athlete.

retardation and preventive care, these measures alone will not be able to overtake the new rise in cases of this disability due to AIDS or babies born of substance-abusing parents.

With the natural progression of better medical care, we as a population are growing older and staying alive longer, including adults with mental retardation. This brings up new questions about what services older adults with developmental disabilities will require.

The disabled rights movement seeks to secure acceptance in society for people with disabilities. The movement works toward securing for the disabled the basic rights and privileges taken for granted by the general population, including: the right to participate

in everyday social, educational and recreational situations; the ability to live side-by-side with other people in normal neighborhood settings; and full integration into the community with resources to allow for continued intellectual and social development.

We're come a long way and we have a long way to go. The complex issues surrounding mental retardation would probably require another book. The purpose of this book is to show the difference that love, patience, training and opportunity can make in the quality of life of the developmentally disabled and to increase awareness of how Special Olympics has helped make a difference.

You can help make a difference. Volunteering with Special Olympics could help make a difference in your life—increasing the quality of your life by the exchange of a spirit of friendship. If you volunteer, you'll understand better than you have ever understood before that all people, including people with mental retardation, can live together, and have the right to live together, in an environment of equality, respect and acceptance.

And what will Special Olympics look like in 2019—25 years from now? Dennis Schmidt of Indiana Special Olympics sums it up nicely: "I share the same goal as Mrs. Shriver—to be alive and still involved with Special Olympics. Special Olympics will remain as an identifiable stand-alone program, but we will be blended into other existing programs, for example, high school athletic programs and park departments. And the Olympics Games will have a gold medal winner—who was a former Special Olympics athlete."

Some Facts & Figures

- Number of family members in the U.S. involved with Special Olympics: more than one million
- Number of family members around the world involved with Special Olympics: more than two million
- Number of Special Olympics volunteers in the U.S.: 454,000
- Number of Special Olympics volunteers outside the U.S.: 100,000
- Number of coaches in the U.S.: 125,000
- Number of coaches worldwide: 250,000

OPPOSITE: Cathy Shene wearing her swimming medals after competing in the 1985 Summer Games.

NEXT PAGE: Cheering fans respond to the athletes with "you're number one" hand signs.

Appendix

Special Olympics Chapters in the United States

Alabama Special Olympics
880 South Court Street
Montgomery, AL 36104
(205) 242-3383

Alaska Special Olympics
21-410 Second Street
Elmendorft, AK 99506
(907) 753-2182

Arizona Special Olympics
3821 East Wier Avenue
Phoenix, AZ 85040
(602) 470-1080

California Special Olympics
501 Colorado Avenue, Suite 200
Santa Monica, CA 90401
(310) 451-1162

Colorado Special Olympics
1400 South Colorado Boulevard, Suite 400
Denver, CO 80222
(303) 691-3339

Connecticut Special Olympics
50 Whiting Street
Plainville, CT 06062
(203) 747-5338

Delaware Special Olympics
Hudson Center, 501 Ogletown Road, Room 123
Newark, DE 19711
(302) 368-6818

District of Columbia Special Olympics
220 Eye Street NE, Suite 140
Washington, D.C. 20002
(202) 544-7770

*OPPOSITE: Ann Walker is number one during a
local area meet in 1985. Awards ceremonies mirror
the Olympic Games protocols for awards.*

Florida Special Olympics
2639 North Monroe Street, Suite 151A
Tallahassee, FL 32303
(904) 385-8178

Georgia Special Olympics
3772 Pleasantdale Road, Suite 195
Atlanta, GA 30340
(404) 414-9390

Hawaii Special Olympics
1085 South Beretania Street, Suite 200
Honolulu, HI 96814
(808) 531-1888

Idaho Special Olympics
8426 Fairview Avenue
Boise, ID 83704
(208) 323-0482

Illinois Special Olympics
605 East Willow
Normal, IL 61761
(309) 888-2551

Indiana Special Olympics
5648 West 74th Street
Indianapolis, IN 46278
(317) 328-2000

Iowa Special Olympics
4921 Douglas, Suite 1
Des Moines, IA 50310
(515) 278-2513

Kansas Special Olympics
5830 Woodson, Suite 106
Mission, KS 66202
(913) 236-9290

Kentucky Special Olympics
214 West Main Street
Frankfort, KY 40601
(502) 227-7296

Louisiana Special Olympics
200 SW Railroad Avenue
Hammond, LA 70403
(504) 345-6644

Maine Special Olympics
28 School Street
Gorham, ME 04038
(207) 839-6030

Maryland Special Olympics
5020 Campbell Boulevard, Suite F
Baltimore, MD 21236
(410) 931-4100

Massachusetts Special Olympics
450 Maple Street, Cottage 1
Danvers, MA 01937
(508) 774-1501

Michigan Special Olympics
Central Michigan University
Mt. Pleasant, MI 48859
(517) 774-3911

Minnesota Special Olympics
625 Fourth Avenue South, Suite 1430
Minneapolis, MN 55415
(612) 333-0999

Mississippi Special Olympics
202 North 33rd Street
Hattiesburg, MS 39406
(601) 264-7295

Missouri Special Olympics
1907 William Street
Jefferson City, MO 65109
(314) 635-1660

Montana Special Olympics
3300 Third Street
Great Falls, MT 59404
(406) 791-2368

Nebraska Special Olympics
5021 South 24th Street
Omaha, NE 68107
(402) 731-5007

Nevada Special Olympics
3160 South Valley View, Suite 106
Las Vegas, NV 89102
(702) 222-1924

New Hampshire Special Olympics
650 Elm Street, Suite 101
Manchester, NH 03101
(603) 624-1250

New Jersey Special Olympics
242 Old New Brunswick Road
Piscataway, NJ 08854
(908) 562-1500

New Mexico Special Olympics
6600 Palomas NE, Suite 207
Albuquerque, NM 87109
(505) 856-0342

New York Special Olympics
Airport Park, 3 Cornell Road
Latham, New York 12110
(518) 786-8661

North Carolina Special Olympics
3209 Bresham Lake Road, Suite 114
Raleigh, NC 27615
(919) 878-7978

North Dakota Special Olympics
2616 South 26th Street
Grand Forks, ND 58201
(701) 746-0331

Ohio Special Olympics
3303 Winchester Pike
Columbus, OH 43232
(614) 239-7050

Oklahoma Special Olympics
6835 South Canton Avenue
Tulsa, OK 74136
(918) 481-1234

Oregon Special Olympics
3325 NW Yeon Avenue
Portland, OR 97210
(503) 248-0600

Pennsylvania Special Olympics
124 Washington Square,
2570 Boulevard of the Generals
Norristown, PA 19403
(215) 630-9450

Rhode Island Special Olympics
33 College Hill Road
Warwick, RI 02886
(401) 823-7411

South Carolina Special Olympics
2615 Devine Street
Columbia, SC 29205
(803) 254-7774

South Dakota Special Olympics
4200 South Louise Avenue, Suite 201
Sioux Falls, SD 57106
(605) 361-2114

Tennessee Special Olympics
112 21st Avenue South, Suite 101
Nashville, TN 37203
(615) 322-8292

Texas Special Olympics
11442 North Interstate 35
Austin, TX 78753
(512) 835-9873

Utah Special Olympics
4 Triad Center, Suite 105
Salt Lake City, UT 84180
(801) 363-1111

Vermont Special Olympics
5 Avenue D
Williston, VT 05495
(802) 863-5222

Virginia Special Olympics
100 West Franklin Street, Suite 400
Richmond, VA 23220
(804) 644-0071

Washington Special Olympics
2150 North 107th Avenue, Suite 220
Seattle, WA 98133
(206) 362-4949

West Virginia Special Olympics
914 Market Street, Suite 201
Parkersburg, WV 26101
(304) 422-1868

Wisconsin Special Olympics
5900 Monona Drive, Suite 301
Madison, WI 53716
(608) 222-1324

Wyoming Special Olympics
341 East E Street, Suite 180
Casper, WY 82601
(307) 235-3062

NEXT TWO PAGES: Special athlete Carol Nordholm and a friend are the guests of Billy Crystal and Danny DeVito on the set of their movie, "Throw Mama From the Train."

Index

Y

Other Books Published by Foghorn Press
CALL (800) FOGHORN (364-4676) TO ORDER

California Hiking: The Complete Guide
by Tom Stienstra & Michael Hodgson
$17.95, 832 pp, 5 3/8 x 8 3/8"

Southwest Camping: The Complete Guide
with Dave Ganci
$14.95, 450 pp, 5 3/8 x 8 3/8"

California Camping: The Complete Guide
by Tom Stienstra
$17.95, 832 pp, 5 3/8 x 8 3/8"

**Pacific Northwest Camping:
The Complete Guide**
by Tom Stienstra
$16.95, 740 pp, 5 3/8 x 8 3/8"

**Rocky Mountain Camping:
The Complete Guide**
by Tom Stienstra
$14.95, 512 pp, 5 3/8 x 8 3/8"

**The California Dog Lover's Companion:
The Inside Scoop on Where to Take Your
Dog in California**
by Maria Goodavage, illustrated by Phil Frank
$16.95, 832 pp, 5 3/8 x 8 3/8"

**The Dog Lover's Companion:
The Inside Scoop on Where to Take Your
Dog in the Bay Area & Beyond**
by Lyle York & Maria Goodavage
illustrated by Phil Frank
$12.95, 320 pp, 5 3/8 x 8 3/8"

California Golf: The Complete Guide
with Mark Soltau
$17.95, 800 pp, color insert, 5 3/8 x 8 3/8"

Hawaii Golf: The Complete Guide
by George Fuller
$16.95, 408 pp, color insert, 5 3/8 x 8 3/8"

California Fishing: The Complete Guide
by Tom Stienstra
$19.95, 768 pp, 5 3/8 x 8 3/8"

California Spas & Urban Retreats
by Laurel Cook
$14.95, 432 pp, 5 3/8 x 8 3/8"

**Great Outdoor Getaways
to the Bay Area and Beyond**
by Tom Stienstra
$14.95, 348 pp, 5 3/8 x 8/38"

**Epic Trips of the West:
Tom Stienstra's 10 Best**
by Tom Stienstra
$9.95, 232 pp, 5 3/8 x 8 3/8"

California Thrill Sports
by Erik Fair
$14.95, 360 pp, color insert, 5 3/8 x 8 3/8"

Great Outdoor Adventures of Hawaii
by Rick Carroll
$12.95, 304 pp, color insert, 5 3/8 x 8 3/8"

**Our Endangered Parks: What You Can Do
to Protect Our National Heritage**
National Parks and Conservation Association
$10.95, 320 pp, 5 3/8 x 8 3/8"

**The Camper's Companion: The Pack-
Along Guide for Better Outdoor Trips**
by Rick Greenspan and Hal Kahn
$12.95, 464 pp, illustrated, 5 3/8 x 8 3/8"

**America's Secret Recreation Areas:
Your Guide to the Forgotten Wild Lands of
the Bureau of Land Management**
by Michael Hodgson
$15.95, 512 pp, color insert, 5 3/8 x 8 3/8"

What Has Made California So Special These Past Twenty Five Years?
Special Olympics

Special Olympics is made up of people. Special Olympics has been changing lives for over 25 years. We celebrate the dedication and skill of those people who have participated in Special Olympics. For those whose lives have already been enriched by Special Olympics, this is a promise that these opportunities will be maintained and expanded. For the thousands of children and adults with mental retardation who have yet to benefit from Special Olympics, together we pledge that the Special Olympics Flame of Hope will be extended to them.

If you would like to join in this pledge of outreach, please write to me or complete the information below and send it to me at:

Special Olympics, California
501 Colorado Street, Suite 200
Santa Monica, CA 90401

Thank You!

Rafer Johnson

Special Olympics Opportunity

I would like to join you in your outreach efforts by:

_____ Registering as an athlete

_____ Volunteering

_____ Making a donation

_____ Receiving more information

_____ Other

Name: _____

Address: _____

City: _____ State: _____ Zip: _____

Telephone: _____